LIVERPOOL:
WORLD HERITAGE CITY

CONTENTS

Cover image supplied by McCoy Wynne Photography

FOREWORD

In 2004 the heart of Liverpool was inscribed by UNESCO as a World Heritage site. This was in response to a nomination submitted by the United Kingdom Government but driven vigorously from within Liverpool and with the City Council's unqualified support. This supreme accolade affords indisputable endorsement for the pre-eminence of Liverpool's historic environment. Yet today, Liverpool is on UNESCO's list of World Heritage in danger.

By recognising the intrinsic qualities of Liverpool's great historic assets, and nurturing them as part of the city's future, that risk can be removed. Liverpool's exceptionalism has been a source of wonder throughout her history, the root of the city's pride and self-esteem, the source of her wealth and the reason why she stands today as England's finest Victorian city. Those decisive virtues represent an astonishing endowment, not only in their own right but as part of the essential fuel needed to animate and sustain the city's future – cultural as well as economic.

Letting this inheritance slip away, through ignorance or neglect, will leave a city profoundly impoverished. Some have implied that to cherish this legacy represents a brake upon change, an obstacle to creating a dynamic city fit for the twenty-first century. But this fails to recognise that the historic environment, properly nurtured, can itself be a powerful engine of inspiration and prosperity, reinforcing identity and the distinctive character that sets Liverpool apart from other cities.

Today, throughout the world enlightened cities recognise the huge benefits that derive from protecting and cherishing their historic treasures and using them as the foundation for a prosperous and vigorous future. To reconcile these potent voices of the past with the needs of today and tomorrow requires understanding, a determination to demand of new developments standards that complement and reinforce the qualities of what has gone before, and the courage to stand by those principles.

Here lies the key to the Liverpool of tomorrow, a city with its eyes set firmly on the future while cherishing the richness of its past.

Sir Neil Cossons OBE
Former Chairman of English Heritage

THE WORLD
HERITAGE CITY

Liverpool Cityscape, commissioned by National Museums Liverpool from the artist Ben Johnson for the European Capital of Culture year 2008

Why is Liverpool a World Heritage Site? In 2004, when the designation was first approved, an anonymous contributor to The Economist (a London based business magazine) was utterly sceptical. London, he argued, had a much better case for such an honour; doubtless he was writing at a desk not far from Piccadilly.

Yet it is a perfectly reasonable question. A most eloquent answer comes from the historian Professor Jack Simmons, writing in 1979, many years before the world heritage badge was first mooted. Liverpool, Simmons argued: 'has a quality to be found in the same abundance nowhere else in England: the quality of grandeur. There are of course English buildings and streets here and there that can truly be called grand – what could be grander than St. Paul's Cathedral? But St. Paul's stands in isolated magnificence; there is nothing else like it in scale or character in London… the quality appears abroad, though less often than you might think: at Lyon, Amiens and Laon, at Antwerp and Wurzberg, in Rome, and repeatedly in Spain'.

Liverpool's Pier Head, completed c.1919, and Shanghai's Bund, completed 1935: today the two cities are twinned

So there you have one personal explanation for Liverpool's exceptional quality: architectural splendour, grandeur, and scale in townscape and topography. Truly it is all a consequence of the city's site on the broad Mersey Estuary, with development rising in terraces above it, in the powerful dock buildings, in the width of the streets, in the twin cathedrals and great civic buildings.

Quentin Hughes, once Professor of Architecture at the University of Liverpool, would have shared this view. In his timeless written and photographic essay Seaport (almost a love letter to his city) Hughes said that Liverpool, for all its fall from power and prominence, remained a world city. It looked out across the Atlantic, linked to the Americas and the Eastern Trade, not parochial and introverted like Yorkshire towns, or gritty, aggressive and hard like its near neighbour Manchester.

Others have agreed. In 1796 Lord Erskine described the young city as: 'this quondam village, which is now fit to be a proud capital for any empire in the world'. Earlier (in 1680) Daniel Defoe had cut to the chase: 'Liverpool is one of the wonders of Britain'. Perhaps, as Quentin Hughes averred, this was a slight exaggeration.

Hughes and Simmons could not avoid emotional entanglement. 'In this paradoxical city' said Hughes 'the feeling is still in the air…the atmosphere is by turns pure and fresh and limpid so that the pinnacles of the Liver Buildings stand out across the silver streak of the river'. Yet emotions are not always sweet. Grandeur, Simmons realised, may have little to do with beauty, and there are many aspects of Liverpool which are ugly and heart-breaking. Poverty abounds here. 'Some people hate Liverpool' he concluded, 'but if you have never seen it you must go there and take it in, without illusions. The experience is unforgettable for the eye and the heart'.

Accept that the fabric, the site, the buildings have a special, even a unique quality. In itself that would certainly not be sufficient justification for world heritage. There are more profound reasons; and these are all to do with Liverpool's relationship with the past, with innovation and with the shaping of world history, sometimes good, sometimes bad (we consider them later). It may seem an exaggeration to describe Liverpool as a city which changed the world. But it is.

A list of Liverpool firsts is now emblazoned on the wall of the city's Central Library. Not all of these relate to its world heritage; but many do. Liverpool had the world's first enclosed commercial wet dock. Its walls still remain, carefully preserved below the Liverpool One shopping centre. You may visit if you wish. These walls seem like the ruins of some vanished civilisation. But they are just the opposite. They are the foundations of a civilisation – a capitalist civilisation, a globalised and industrial society – which has spread across and now dominates the world, even in Communist China and post-Communist Russia. It started here, with Liverpool as Ostia to Manchester's Rome.

The Liverpool and Manchester Railway was the first passenger-carrying railway in the world between two cities. Here is a technical innovation of the first rank, as important in its way and in its day as the electronic computer – and maybe more so. It is still in everyday use, and is integral to transport systems and economic prosperity worldwide.

Liverpool led the way in building construction with some of the earliest iron framed buildings in the world by the unsung architect Peter Ellis. Ellis was derided in his day and quickly disappeared from history, but his buildings are still in everyday use. More than this – it appears that these startling neologisms were seen and picked up by Chicago's architects, thus setting the stage for steel-framed skyscrapers and the rise of modernist architecture. For the Chicago architect John W Root had been evacuated in the civil war to Liverpool, and must have seen Peter Ellis's Oriel Chambers and 16 Cook Street, the pioneer cast iron buildings.

There were other firsts, some recognised explicitly by the world heritage status, others less so. With Sir Basil Mott and Sir Maurice Fitzmaurice, James Brodie, the dynamic pre-war City Engineer, was responsible for the greatest engineering feat of the 1930s in the two mile long Mersey road tunnel. Connecting Liverpool and Birkenhead, it was the longest underwater road tunnel in the world, a giant sinuous single 44 ft. diameter bore, with provision for two lanes of traffic in each direction. Originally lined with a Vitrolite black glass dado, framed in stainless steel, and with six monumental ventilation shafts by the architect Herbert Rowse, this was (and remains) a supremely confident and glamorous expression of municipal power and ability. Clearly a man of many parts, Brodie was also the inventor of football nets.

The world's first commercial enclosed wet dock, 1715

The world's first passenger railway line between Liverpool and Manchester, 1830

The goal net, invented by John Brodie, City Engineer and first used at Stanley Park, Liverpool, 1889

The world's first overhead electric railway, 1893

Construction work on the Mersey Tunnel 12th March 1930

Chinese urban planners in Liverpool with the City's former World Heritage Officer

Chinese Paifang in Nelson Street, Liverpool's Chinatown

Liverpool University, funded by the soap magnate Lord Leverhulme, created the world's first town planning school, the Department of Civic Design, in 1909. It is still going strong, although these days the great majority of students on its masters courses are Chinese rather than British. China it seems believes in planning; perhaps that is one reason why it is the fastest growing and most dynamic country in the world. Whatever the truth, it is another example of Liverpool influencing and shaping the world through innovation; and, as the Chinese students return home, how it continues to do so today. Incidentally Liverpool's Chinatown was the first in Europe and, continuing the international connection, the Liverpool School of Tropical Medicine was the first in the UK. It remains a world class institution, with international funding and status, including recent support from the Bill and Melinda Gates Foundation.

There is one Liverpool connection to the wider world which will forever be ugly and heart-breaking. It has to be faced up to: the slave trade. The Portuguese were the first to capture native Africans and forcibly transport them for labour in the 15th century. Other European nations soon followed, the earliest examples in Britain being London and Bristol merchants. By the mid 18th century Liverpool merchants dominated the trade; between 1699 and 1807 they transported over one million slaves in 5,249 voyages, establishing a triangular trade pattern, whereby manufactured goods were taken to Africa, slaves to the Americas and the Caribbean, and sugar and cotton as raw materials to Britain. Much of the wealth that built Georgian Liverpool in and around Rodney Street (outside the World Heritage Site) and the Town Hall (within it) originated from this immoral trade, which was abolished in Britain in 1807. It was not abolished in British colonies until 1833.

The human consequences have been profound, not just in the misery of the slaves, but in their eventual liberation and subsequent struggle for civil rights. Michelle Obama is descended from slaves. So too are the musicians who created jazz, soul and the blues, from Louis Armstrong, through Leadbelly, Duke Ellington, Stevie Wonder and Miles Davis. Ellington spoke movingly and prophetically in 1931: 'The music of my race is the result of our transplantation to American soil and was our reaction, in plantation days, to the life we lived. What we could not say openly we expressed in music… I think the music of my race is something that is going to live, something which posterity will honour in a higher sense than merely that of the music of the ballroom'.

American black music, especially the blues, is the essential foundation stone for modern music. Rock and Roll, created by Elvis Presley in Memphis Tennessee, fused together the separate traditions of country music and the delta blues. Country music in turn has its origins in the music and culture of white settlers who had migrated to America from Scotland, Ulster and the North of England. They were rough and clannish types, speaking in an earthy dialect. Sexual processes and natural functions were freely used in their figurative expressions. Causing a great deal of trouble with the Quakers, they moved to the high lands of Appalachia. Like countless others, they would have started their voyage from Liverpool.

During the 19th century Liverpool dominated European emigration to the United States. Of 5.5 million emigrants who crossed the Atlantic from Britain, 4.75 million sailed from Liverpool. Of the 482,829 emigrants who sailed from continental Europe in 1887, 199,441 sailed from Liverpool. Few if any other port cities can have had such a profound effect on the lives of so many.

© John 'Hoppy' Hopkins

The Beatles conquer America, 1964

During the 1960s a new cultural traffic flowed back to Liverpool from America. Merchant seamen and especially the 'Cunard Yanks' – crews on Liverpool's Atlantic liners – brought back to Liverpool the music of black musicians, otherwise unheard in Britain, as vinyl singles, exposing a new generation of young white musicians to the music, amongst them two Liverpool schoolboys – Paul McCartney and John Lennon. In Lennon's words: 'It was black music we all dug – we listened to Sleepy John Estes. We can sing more coloured than the Africans'. Lennon did have a reputation for overstating it. Yet the rest is history. The Beatles are mentioned in the world heritage site's statement of outstanding universal value, though their debt to others is not.

The criteria under which Liverpool's inscription for world heritage status was proposed drily reflects its tumultuous history: 'the nominated site exhibits an important interchange of human values over a span of time; Liverpool is the supreme example of a commercial port at the time of Britain's greatest global influence; the site bears a unique or exceptional testimony to a cultural tradition or civilisation'. Indeed so. The more recent Statement of Outstanding Universal Value, reproduced at the end of this book, sets out the full rationale in official prose. Correctly, it majors on cultural impact and historic significance, rather than views, architecture and built forms. Indeed there is but fleeting reference to these issues.

Yet it is the physical environment, and especially long distance views of the city, which is at the centre of recent controversy. UNESCO's missions have been to Liverpool twice. First they came in 2006 to consider, and ultimately to accept, the new Museum of Liverpool and the nearby black Mann Island buildings at the Pier Head. They came again in 2011 to consider proposals for tall buildings north of the Pier Head, in the so called Liverpool Waters development, part of which is in the World Heritage Site, but much of which is outside. The Liverpool Waters proposal now has outline planning permission. As a result, essentially because of the potential impact of these buildings on long distance views of the World Heritage Site and the areas close to it, UNESCO has placed the city on its list of World Heritage Sites In Danger. It may be many years before the tall buildings are built, and there is ample time for further discussion, modification and reflection. Of course, there is nothing intrinsically wrong with new buildings in Liverpool's townscape. It has the topography and resilience to accept big developments and take them in its stride – as it has with the two cathedrals, dominating the sandstone ridge, the St John's Beacon, the Liverpool One development, and indeed the Albert Dock, which was hated in its day by some. 'The works for strength and durability are unsurpassable, but it is regretted that no attention whatsoever has been paid to beauty as well as strength. The enormous pile of warehouses which looms so large upon the river and in its vastness surpasses the pyramid of Cheops is simply a hideous pile of naked brick work'. That was Sir James Picton, Liverpool's historian, reacting to the new Albert Dock in 1873. Few would agree with his strictures today.

In 1972 UNESCO adopted the Convention Concerning the Protection of the World Cultural and Natural Heritage. This recognises that there are places of Outstanding Universal Value to all humanity, which may be at increasing risk of decay and destruction, where the international community has a collective responsibility to protect and promote their value. All nations which have ratified the Convention (the UK did this in 1984) are able to nominate such places for inscription on the World Heritage List. The World Heritage Committee, whose 21 member countries are elected from the 192 states that have ratified the Convention, decides whether nominations should be entered on the World Heritage List. World Heritage Site status places responsibility on national governments to protect and manage World Heritage properties effectively, and if the World Heritage Committee is particularly concerned that a property is at risk, it may place the site on the List of World Heritage in Danger (as a catalyst for remedial action) or even delete it from the World Heritage List. There are now over 1000 World Heritage Sites across the planet; Liverpool was inscribed as a supreme example of a maritime mercantile city in 2004.

The reasons why UNESCO has agreed that Liverpool is of outstanding universal value are:

-Liverpool played a leading role in the development of dock construction, port management and international trading systems in the 18th and 19th centuries.
-The buildings and structures of the port and the city are an exceptional testimony to mercantile culture.
-Liverpool played a major role in influencing globally significant demographic changes in the 18th and 19th centuries, both through its role in the transatlantic slave trade and as the leading port of mass European emigration to the New World.

This book aims to explain why Liverpool is a World Heritage Site, but to do this it takes a broader look at the city's history, and includes some information that does not relate directly to its World Heritage Site status.

Aerial view of Liverpool 1859

ORIGINS

Liverpool owes its existence to its situation on the east bank of the River Mersey, near the estuary into the Irish Sea. From here the river could be crossed and, more importantly, sea voyages could be made to Ireland, the Americas and beyond. But despite the advantage of the coastal location, giving access to the oceans on the western side of England, the river's swirling eddies and the large tidal range of up to 10 metres made it a hazardous port of call. For the port to succeed, it had to find ways of providing safe moorings and shelter for vessels. It managed to do so through the construction of a system of enclosed docks, and during the 18th and 19th centuries the success of the port was paralleled by the spectacular growth of the city. Vast quantities and varieties of goods passed through the docks, helping Great Britain to become the world's first industrial nation and making Liverpool a centre of mercantile transactions across the globe. The surviving buildings and structures of the historic city make it the supreme example of a commercial port of the 18th, 19th and early 20th centuries.

Loading Reels of BI Cables at the docks in early 20th century

Beginnings as a Ferry Point

Liverpool's first organised maritime activity was the ferry across the wide River Mersey. Birkenhead Priory was founded on the west side of the river about 1150 and it is thought that the monks ran an irregular ferry service to the small settlement on the east side. Certainly, in 1318 the monks were granted ferry rights by Edward II. Liverpool was first mentioned as Liuerpool in a charter of Prince John of around 1192. The settlement was concentrated in the area which is now roughly between Water Street, Castle Street, James Street and The Strand (which was then the river bank). A tidal pool ran inland immediately to the south of the settlement, where a small stream flowed into the Mersey. One school of thought holds that this pool within the natural bedrock of red sandstone gave the name to the settlement. At high tide the pool became an inlet approximately 1.5 km long, where ships could enter and gain protection from the hostile river currents. But at low tide the pool became a muddy expanse where ships would keel over unless propped, making it far from ideal as a harbour. Even so, the Pool was an important factor in the town's early life, where cargoes were loaded and unloaded, passengers could board and alight, and ships could be built and repaired.

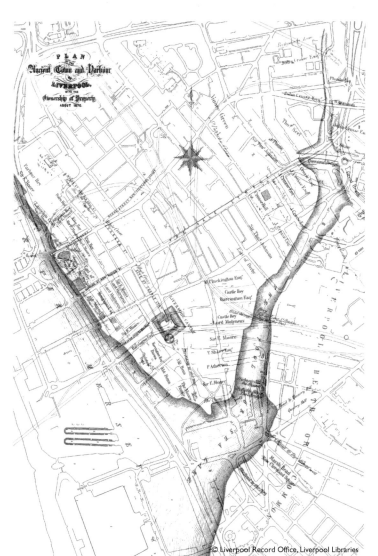

Plan of Pool of Liverpool circa 1670 overlain on street plan circa 2002

Until the introduction of steam boats the operation of a regular cross-river ferry service was largely dependent on favourable wind and tide. The Elizabeth, a steam-powered ferry was introduced in 1815 to take people to Runcorn, where they could then take the canal packet boat to Manchester. The Etna, introduced in 1817 was the first Liverpool-Birkenhead steam-powered ferry and transformed the voyage. By 1844, there were many steam ferries in operation from a variety of terminals on the Wirral. The Mersey Ferries still operate today both as a commuter service and for leisure cruises and are the best way to see Liverpool's World Heritage Site waterfront.

Rock Ferry ferry boat by Samuel Walters

Original Seven Street of Liverpool

Royal Foundation as a base to sail to Wales and Ireland

King John formally established Liverpool with the grant of a Charter in 1207. Eight years before he signed the Magna Carta of 1215, the king needed a convenient port of embarkation to enable him to mount his expansion into Wales and Ireland. Chester was the larger port at that time but it was under the control of the powerful and independent Earl of Chester and so John obtained possession of Liverpool and issued a Charter inviting settlers, promising privileges in land holding and freedom from dues as an inducement. The Charter was significant in superimposing a royal trading and semi-military regime on what had been a predominantly farming and fishing community, and provided labour for the port. Although Liverpool was to become a commercial port, its origins are royal and military.

Seven main streets were created following 1207: what are now Castle Street, Old Hall Street, Chapel Street, Water Street, Dale Street, High Street and Tithebarn Street. The seven streets give their name to a popular cultural website:

http://www.sevenstreets.com. They were laid out in the form of a letter "H" with an extended cross-bar, the River Mersey forming the western boundary of the town, along the line of the current The Strand, and the Pool marked the southern boundary.

It is sometimes said flippantly that '...not much happened in the first 500 years of Liverpool.' It is true that from 1207 until 1700 few important additions were made to the original street plan, but significant buildings were soon erected and as the 17th century progressed Liverpool's international trading voyages steadily increased. For most of that half-millennium, Liverpool's waterfront was dominated by three substantial landmarks (Liverpool Castle, The Tower of Liverpool and the Church of St. Nicholas and Our Lady), which were all related to its maritime location.

Liverpool Castle

To defend the new town, a castle was built early in the 13th century on a rocky ledge of higher ground, now partially occupied by Derby Square and the Queen Victoria Monument. The last remains of the castle above ground were removed

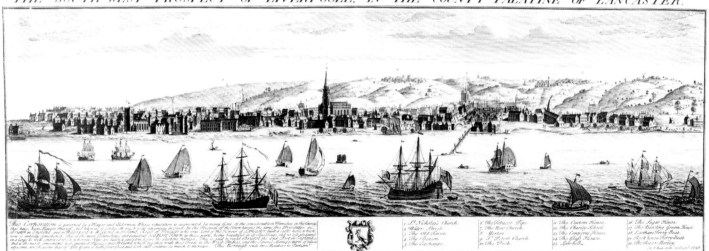

Buck's 1728 drawing of Liverpool's waterfront

in 1726, when it was replaced by St. George's Church (also now demolished), although there is a plaque to commemorate it on the Victoria Monument. The brutalist concrete edifice of the Queen Elizabeth II Crown Courts (1984) gives some impression of the scale and dominance of the castle.

The Tower of Liverpool

The Stanley family is a prominent local dynasty which had estates on the Isle of Man from 1405. The possession of the Isle of Man made a military base in Liverpool highly desirable and so in 1406 Sir John Stanley was authorised by Henry IV to fortify the Tower of Liverpool and it became the second military stronghold in the town on the current site of Tower Buildings at the bottom of Water Street. The Tower passed out of the ownership of the Stanleys in 1717 and was used for a time as a gaol, but it was eventually pulled down in 1819.

Map of Liverpool, The River Mersey and the Wirral 1577

Churches of St. Mary del Quay and St. Nicholas

A stone chapel of St Mary del Quay was in existence by 1257 on a rocky platform just above the waterline and St. Nicholas Chapel was built within the same churchyard in 1355. The present church is dedicated to Our Lady and St. Nicholas and has been rebuilt in stages on several occasions, with the nave only completed in 1952 after wartime damage. It is still known locally as 'the sailors' church and has a ship for its weathervane.

Irish Trade and Scottish Trade

The geographical relationship of Ireland with the west coast of England generated a longstanding pattern of trading across the Irish Sea. In the reign of Henry VIII there is a record of 27 vessels entering and leaving the port in three months, bringing Irish yarn, sheep and deer skins, tanned and salted hides and tallow. To Ireland went the famous Yorkshire broadcloths, Manchester cottons, Kendal dyed cottons, Sheffield cutlery, coarse stockings, blankets and sailcloth. The import of Irish cattle did not begin until 1665. By that time Ireland was taking thousands of tons of coal, thousands of bushels of salt, as well as tobacco and sugar from Liverpool. Likewise, the geographical relationship of Liverpool with the west coast of Scotland and Wales led to an early coastal shipping trade, avoiding the need for difficult long land journeys.

Liverpool's longstanding trading connections with Ireland Scotland and Wales have resulted in continued strong Irish, Scottish and Welsh communities and have influenced the city's distinctive cultural identity.

Statue of Christopher Columbus at Sefton Park Palm House with the inscription: 'The discoverer of America was the maker of Liverpool'.

Rivalry between Chester and Liverpool

Liverpool had a long running rivalry with the nearby port of Chester on the River Dee. In 1565, the merchants of Chester described Liverpool as 'a creek of the port of Chester' and in 1580 they tried to claim the right to control Liverpool's trade with Spain and Portugal. The dispute was resolved by the Master of the Rolls and the Lord Chief Justice who ruled that 'suche poore cities and townes' as Liverpool should not be excluded from trade. As the River Dee began to silt up, Liverpool's share of trade gradually grew and by 1670, 110 vessels were trading from Liverpool compared with 30 from Chester and five from other ports on the Lancashire coast.

One factor which had hampered mercantile activity in Liverpool had been the trade restrictions imposed by the burgesses under their charter right. For trade to be able to expand significantly, it was necessary for the customs due to the Crown and the town to be collected. This was initially done from the Town Hall, but after a new Town Hall was built in 1673-4 a purpose-designed Custom House was erected in Moor Street in 1688.

The Beginning of Trans-Atlantic Trade

Early town books from the mid-16th century provide a record of cargoes from Spain, Portugal and France, and it was a Liverpool merchant, Humphrey Brooke, who brought the first news that the Spanish Armada had put to sea in 1588. Around the middle of the 17th century Liverpool merchants began to develop trade with America, and once established, it expanded rapidly, to mutual benefit. Indeed a statue of Columbus outside the Palm House in Sefton Park bears a plaque 'The discoverer of America was the maker of Liverpool'.

The first recorded American cargo to arrive consisted of 30 tons of tobacco, brought by James Jenkinson in the Friendship, in 1648. The discovery of the American continent and the formation of the British West Indian colonies heralded a new era of trade. The new colonies wanted English goods in exchange for their products, and of the English ports, Liverpool benefited most because of its proximity to the growing industrial areas of Lancashire, Yorkshire and Staffordshire, and to the salt from Cheshire.

The rise in fortunes of Liverpool owed much to the shrewdness of the new generation of merchants who sought their own personal profit and who combined with each other to collectively finance the facilities of the port.

Seventeenth Century Growth of the Town

The English Civil War had restricted Liverpool's growth in the mid 17th century, but after the Restoration of the Monarchy in 1660 there was a rapid recovery. In 1665 sugar refining was established in a building off Dale Street as a result of the start of the West Indian Trade. The greatest trade in any one single cargo was the import of tobacco, mostly from Virginia. A 1727 view of Liverpool shows a Tobacco Pipe right on the waterfront, approximately at the bottom of the current Brunswick Street. The import of tobacco had risen from almost nothing in 1665 to 1.75 million pounds in 1699, and sugar from 700 cwt. to 11,600 cwt. In the same period exports of salt grew from 6,000 bushels to 300,000. By 1702, Liverpool was the third trading port in England, behind London and Bristol. It had 102 vessels averaging 85 tons and 1,101 seamen, compared with Bristol's 165 vessels averaging 105 tons and 2,389 seamen, and London's 560 vessels, averaging 105 tons and 10,065 seamen.

By 1698 Liverpool had 24 streets, and a population of about 6,000. Celia Fiennes, described it that year as 'London in miniature...with long, handsome, well paved streets lined by…houses of brick and stone built high and even. It was very rich with an abundance of persons...very well dressed and of good fashion.'

Detail from Buck's 1728 drawing showing Old Dock from the river, with Ripley's Custom House on east quay

Early Dock Facilities and the First Enclosed Dock

At intervals throughout the 17th Century, the Town Council had spent money to maintain the harbour in the Pool, and in 1665 a new quay was built, probably along the Strand on the Mersey itself. In 1702, however, shipowners expressed dissatisfaction with the adequacy of the mooring facilities and the dangers caused by the overcrowded moorings in the river and pool. Ships were visiting the port from many parts of the world, and the poem A Trip to Leverpoole, published in London in 1706, gives some indication of the changing status of the town:

'At length to Leverpoole we came…
And any man alive who'd guess,
By the Town's sudden rise, no less:
From a small Fishery of late,
Became the darling child of Fate;
So wealthy grown, so full of Hurry,
That she eclipses Bristol's Glory.'

Such was the increase in shipping and the inadequacy of the port facilities to accommodate further growth that the town took the most important step since its foundation. It resolved to seek permission through a 1709 Act of Parliament, to construct a permanent wet dock – the first such commercial enclosed dock in the world. It was the first of many such local Acts of Parliament over the next 150 years which resulted in the construction of 21 docks before 1857, when the Mersey Docks and Harbour Board was established to take responsibility for Liverpool's docks. The driving force behind the construction of the first dock was Sir Thomas Johnson (after whom Sir Thomas Street was named), a leading local politician and merchant. The engineer for the project was Thomas Steers. It was opened in 1715 and was the catalyst for Liverpool's subsequent rise to the status of a world port. The opening of Old Dock, as it became known, and each subsequent dock, facilitated further massive increases in the number of ships based in Liverpool, those visiting and the volume and profit of trade. In 1709, Liverpool's 84 ships had a capacity of 5,789 tons but by 1737, the number of Liverpool owned ships had grown to 171, with a capacity of 12,016 tons. It was the bold decision to construct the world's first commercial enclosed wet dock that propelled Liverpool's rise to become one of the greatest commercial seaports in the world.

Slave ship

The Trans-Atlantic Slave Trade

The slave trade across the Atlantic Ocean represents the largest-ever enforced deportation of humanity. It is estimated that from the middle of the 15th century to the end of the 19th century, more than twelve million Africans were taken forcibly from their homes to the New World. In the 18th century alone, six million enslaved Africans reached the American plantations. Great Britain had the most powerful of the slave trading fleets in the 17th, 18th and very early years of the 19th centuries, as the growth of plantations in the West Indies and English mainland America provided the greatest impetus to the slave trade.

It was a triangular operation, with ships sailing from England to Africa with a wide range of manufactured items. There, those goods were exchanged with African dealers for slaves whom they had captured and who were packed into the holds, manacled together in appalling conditions for the middle passage across the Atlantic, which could take 50-60 days. The inhumane conditions resulted in incalculable suffering and many deaths. The slaves were taken to the sugar plantations of the West Indies or the southern colonies of America, where they were sold to provide unpaid labour and where they endured lives of great hardship often on the estates of British colonists. Meanwhile, the ships were loaded up with natural produce such as sugar, rum, cotton, mahogany and tobacco, and brought back to England. Profits were made on each of the three legs and it could be a highly lucrative business for the ship owners and investors. Slaves were rarely brought to England, but the profits from the trade were brought back and provided much of the financial capital for the continued growth of Liverpool's port facilities.

Although the earliest record of a slaving ship, The Blessing, trading from Liverpool appears in papers of 1700, the merchants of Liverpool were initially slow to take a major role in the slave trade. As the 18th century progressed, however, Liverpool merchants became increasingly involved and by the latter half of the century had become the leading exponents. During the city's involvement over 1,360,000 African captives were transported in over 5,000 voyages of ships based in Liverpool. By contrast in the same period, 740,000 slaves were taken

in just over 2,000 voyages by London-based ships, the second slave trading-port of this country. More than half of all the slaves sold by English traders were from Liverpool. Indeed, in the latter years of the 18th century, Liverpool had upwards of 70% of the nation's slave trade.

Attitudes towards slavery varied a great deal. Men such as Wilberforce, Pitt and Fox campaigned vociferously for abolition, but were opposed by many Liverpool merchants. Liverpool did have a small but influential circle of abolitionists, who formed their own branch of the Society of Abolition. In 1788, its subscribers included doctors (Dr James Currie and Dr Jonathan Binns), Quakers (Daniel Daulby and William Rathbone), a preacher (John Yates), a former sea captain (John Newton), a former sailor (Edward Rushton) and perhaps most famously William Roscoe.

Portrait of William Roscoe 1819 by Sir Martin Archer Shee

Roscoe was a man of many talents and one of Liverpool's greatest sons. He was a successful lawyer, banker, botanist, poet, writer, agricultural pioneer and a collector of Italian manuscripts and paintings. In the 1780s he wrote and published a two-part epic poem *The Wrongs of Africa*, and he had considerable influence on the national attitude through his literary works. In 1806, Roscoe was elected Member of Parliament for Liverpool, and after 30 years of campaigning, he successfully supported the Abolition Bill of 1807 to outlaw the transportation of slaves by British ships. The use of slave labour in British colonies was finally ended in 1836.

Liverpool thus played a major role in changing the demographics and culture of the world's population. Liverpool City Council has publicly apologised on behalf of the city for its role in the slave trade, the city participates in Slavery Remembrance Day every year on 23rd August and National Museums Liverpool has established the International Slavery Museum.

Eighteenth Century Civic Improvements

The opportunities in business and trade drew people to Liverpool from all parts of Britain. The population continued to grow from 5,000 in 1700 to 22,000 in 1750, and then to 56,000 in 1790. By 1801 Liverpool had become the largest town in England.

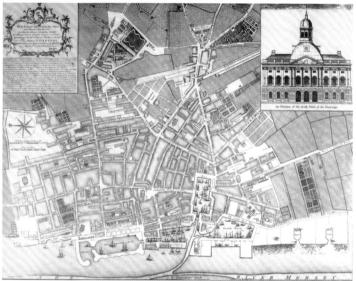

Eyes Map of Liverpool 1765

With increased prosperity came civic responsibilities. The first council treasurer was appointed in 1716, the present (third) Town Hall was opened in 1754, and the first Dock Committee was introduced in 1761. Buck's drawing of the South West Prospect of Liverpool of 1728 gives a good representation of the town at that time. It shows the castle having gone and the most prominent buildings added since 1680 being St. Peter's Church (on the south side of Church Street), consecrated in 1704 and St. George's Church (on Derby Square) completed in 1734. The Bluecoat Charity School on School Lane was completed in 1718, paid for by Bryan Blundell and other Liverpool sea captains. The early 18th-century painting of Liverpool below has some discrepancies with Buck's drawing, but it shows more clearly the construction of the timber pier, the entrance to Old Dock and provides a good view of the Custom House beyond.

A series of 18th century maps (Chadwick's plan of 1725, Eyes' plan of 1765, Perry's plan of 1769 and Eyes' plan of 1785) provides a clear demonstration of the development of Liverpool in that period. In 1791 Lord Erskine declared that 'Liverpool is…fit to be a proud capital of any empire in the world.'

The Improvement of Facilities for the Docks and Transportation

Captain William Hutchinson, a successful Liverpool privateer, was appointed Dock Master in 1759. Under his guidance further improvements were made to Liverpool's docks, not least the construction of George's Dock. He invented the reflecting mirrors for lighthouses, and made observations of high tides at Liverpool twice a day every day for 30 years; his research ultimately leading to the production of Holden's tide tables. He supervised the erection of lighthouses, such as Perch Rock at New Brighton and the introduction of the Liverpool Pilot Service in 1765.

Perch Rock Lighthouse, New Brighton

Although the Old Dock had increased the capacity of the port, further growth was dependent on improvements to the inland transport system. This soon took shape with the construction of canals. The first was the Mersey and Irwell Navigation opened in 1736, followed by the Douglas Navigation in 1742, primarily to enable coal to be brought to Liverpool for use and export, the Sankey Canal in 1759 and the Bridgewater Canal in 1761. In 1770, the first Leeds and Liverpool Canal Act was passed, the Liverpool section being completed by January 1773. It was not until 1816 that whole canal was opened, becoming the longest and ultimately most successful canal in Britain. Much of its success was due to its route, which served areas needing several types of cargo to be brought to and from Liverpool. Wool, cotton, limestone, grain and general cargo were all carried in huge quantities by a wide range of carriers, but the greatest commodity was coal, not only for industrial and domestic use but also for export, particularly to Ireland. In 1794, over 150,000 tons were delivered to the Liverpool terminus, a coal wharf basin at Old Hall Street, which is still marked by the small brick building at the Radisson Hotel.

One of the more exotic commodities, alpaca wool, was taken along the canal to Salts Mill in Saltaire, which is also now a World Heritage Site.

Early 18th century painting of Old Dock from the river, with Ripley's Custom House on east quay

Postcard of the Liverpool Overhead Railway

Painting of Stephenson's Rocket during Rainhill Trials 1829 by Alan Fearnley

Liverpool and Manchester Railway

The idea of a railway between Liverpool and Manchester was first promoted by a group of Liverpool businessmen. The line was complete by June 1830 and was the first inter-city railway in the world to carry passengers as well as goods to regular timetables. When the tunnel through to Lime Street Station was opened in 1836, passengers still had to change carriages at Edge Hill as the Lime Street to Edge Hill section was operated by a static winding engine until 1890. Lime Street Station was the first station in the world to be covered with a roof spanning the tracks.

The opening of the railways enabled goods arriving at and departing from Liverpool Docks to be transported to and from other parts of Great Britain far more efficiently and speedily than before and the port came to depend upon the railways for maintaining its global trading position. Liverpool's early harnessing of railways is a demonstration of its determination to use new technology for commercial gain and enabled the port to prosper.

Liverpool Overhead Railway

The Liverpool Overhead Railway Company was formed in 1888 and building began the following year. The original intention had been for steam traction to be employed, then cable haulage, before electric traction was decided upon. The first train ran in 1892 and it was the world's first elevated electric railway. It ran the full seven miles of the docks and had 17 stations. The overhead railway was a famous sight in Liverpool, providing fascinating views into the docks and became a tourism attraction in its own right. It became known locally as 'The Dockers' Umbrella' and ran until 1956 when severe corrosion was found in parts of the elevated structure and it was later demolished, leaving only a few remaining fragments, such as support columns in the dock wall and a high level tunnel entrance at Herculaneum Dock. A restored carriage and a section of elevated track are on display in the Museum of Liverpool.

The Mersey Railway Tunnel

By the beginning of the 19th century, the Mersey ferries were inadequate to cope with rising demand for cross-river travel and so the practicalities of constructing tunnels to connect the two sides of the river were investigated. In 1866, merchants and industrialists successfully promoted an Act of Parliament to allow the construction of a railway tunnel under the river and on 1st February, 1886 the first passenger steam trains passed through, carrying 36,000 people on that day.

Ventilation of the tunnel was achieved partly by the installation of four large Guibal fans in a special vent passage connected to the pumping and ventilation station at George's Dock. However, these proved to be inadequate to clear the smoke from the huge six-coupled tank locomotives and in 1899 it was decided to electrify the line. This was completed in 1903, when it became the world's first electrified under-water railway.

The Industrial Revolution

The rapid expansion of Liverpool's dock facilities in the 18th and 19th centuries was not only a product of the industrialisation of England, but was also critical to that process. Without the port's capacity to import raw materials and to export manufactured goods, industries across much of England could not have developed as successfully as they did.

© Liverpool Record Office, Liverpool Libraries

Cotton Traders 1922

The textile industry is an example. Between 1700 and 1790, the amount of raw cotton imported increased 50 times and this coincided with changes in production from home-based to factory-based industries with the invention of new types of machinery to speed up the spinning and weaving of cotton. The Lancashire cotton mills took full advantage of the access to supplies of raw cotton from the new America plantations, imported mainly through Liverpool, and also the almost unlimited export market, again via Liverpool. Manchester became the centre of the Lancashire cotton industry and was included on the UK's 1999 Tentative List of World Heritage Sites as 'The Archetype City of the Industrial Revolution'. Liverpool was the main port for Manchester, the conduit for importing raw cotton and exporting finished cloth, until the Manchester Ship Canal was opened in January 1894 and became the largest river navigation canal in the world. It meant that Manchester no longer had to rely on (and pay for) Liverpool's docks and enabled the newly created Port of Manchester to become Britain's third busiest port.

Coal on the Leeds and Liverpool Canal circa 1950

Other industries that made rapid advances in methods and scale of production were iron and steel making. The products, particularly the small-arms and tools from the Midlands and railroad iron bound for America, were an important element of Liverpool's exports.

Coal was vital to the Industrial Revolution as a source of energy, and exports, both to other ports in Britain and abroad. The quantity of coal passing through the port increased ten times between 1770 and 1791. Its importance became even more marked with the widespread introduction of steam power for production machines and transportation. The first steamship entered the Mersey in 1815 and the first transatlantic steamer to complete a crossing from Liverpool was the Royal William in 1833. This heralded a new era for shipping and led to further increases in tonnage going through Liverpool, as ships were no longer dependent upon the weather, but could operate to regular schedules. Nevertheless, more sailing ships than steamships were arriving in the port until well into the second half of the 19th century. From 1813, when the East India Company's monopoly on trade was abolished, until 1857, imports of cotton into Liverpool increased five times, and imports of sugar and rum went up by 50%. In the same period, wheat imports from North America increased tenfold and salt exports went up three times.

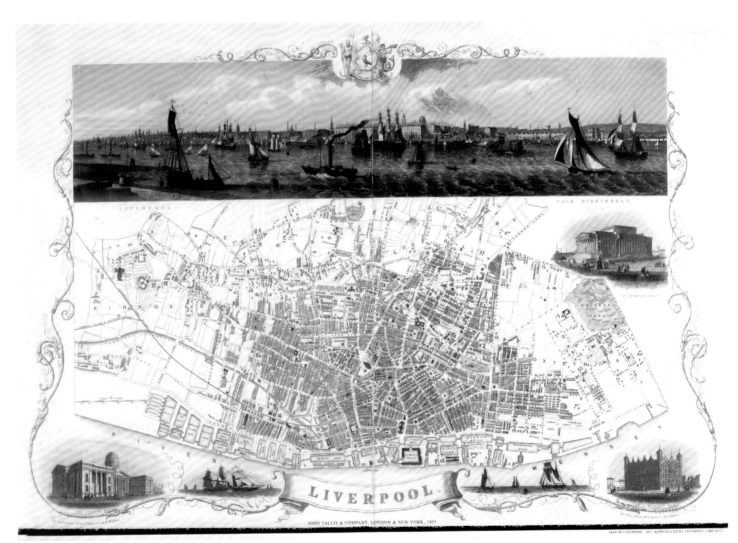

Tallis Map 1851

Liverpool in the Nineteenth Century

The growth of Liverpool – its docks and its mercantile influence upon the world – continued in an even more dramatic fashion in the 19th century. In many ways the growth was a partnership between the Corporation and merchants in an ongoing cycle of expansion. The Dock Committee (and later the Mersey Docks and Harbour Board) organised the construction of the docks, the businessmen managed the expansion of their businesses in the town and across the world, workers were attracted to Liverpool to work, or en route to the New World, and the Corporation provided services for those who stayed.

The population grew even more rapidly in the 19th century; from 78,000 in 1801 to 376,000 in 1851, and to 685,000 in 1901. During this time Liverpool became the most successful embarkation port for mass transatlantic emigration, and following its previous role in the slave trade was thus responsible for two of the world's biggest demographic changes. The prosperity of Liverpool and its role as a point of emigration to the New World attracted thousands upon thousands of people from across Europe. In 1847 alone, 300,000 Irish people were driven to flee to Liverpool to escape the hunger caused partially by the Potato Famine.

Jesse Hartley

Court housing, Liverpool 1930s

Jesse Hartley was appointed Dock Engineer to the Port of Liverpool in 1824 and kept the position until his death in 1860. He was the world's first full-time salaried dock engineer and during his tenure, he either built or altered all of Liverpool's docks of the day and built the landmark warehouses at Albert, Wapping and Stanley Dock. He has had a bigger impact on Liverpool's waterfront than any other individual and whilst his name is well-known, he is barely celebrated in the city.

Until the beginning of the 19th century, most Liverpool traders worked from home in the city centre, and often had a warehouse either attached or adjacent to their house. As the scale of operations expanded and the successful businessmen moved their homes to the healthier fringes of the town, the scale and character of the central area changed. Purely commercial buildings became the external symbols of the mercantile culture, and success and power of business was to transform the main streets from a domestic to monumental scale of grandeur.

Many emigrated but others stayed and added to the cramped and insanitary housing conditions in the courts of central Liverpool. As described by Herman Melville in his semi-autobiographical novel, *Redburn* (1849):
'…the cellars, sinks and hovels of the wretched lanes and courts near the river…. In some parts of the town, inhabited by labourers, and poor people generally, I used to crowd my way through masses of squalid men, women and children who at this evening hour, in those quarters of Liverpool, seem to empty themselves into the street, and live there for the time…..Poverty, poverty, poverty.'

In response to these problems, Liverpool made significant advances in health care. The city appointed the country's first Medical Officer of Health, Dr Duncan, in 1847, opened the first children's hospital in the country in 1851, the first public wash-house in the world in 1842, the first public baths in the country in 1848, appointed Britain's first Borough Engineer, James Newlands, in 1847 and founded the first District Nursing Service in the country in 1855. Dr Duncan wrote in 1842:
'The cellars are underground, having no windows and no communication with the outside air excepting by the door, the top of which is sometimes not higher than the level of the street. When the door of such a cellar is closed, light and air are both excluded. Access to the door is by a narrow flight of steps descending from the street. The roof is so low that a person of moderate height cannot stand upright. There is frequently no floor except the bare earth. There is usually one apartment (10 to 12 square feet) but in some cases there is a back cellar used as a sleeping room…All the cellars are dark, damp, ill-ventilated and dirty. There are upwards of 8,000 inhabited cellars in Liverpool and I estimate their occupants at from 35,000 to 40,000.'

© Liverpool Record Office, Liverpool Libraries

Men outside Custom House circa 1890

The Mersey Docks and Harbour Board

The need for new docks continued throughout the 19th century and a further eight were constructed in Liverpool between 1848 and 1852 as well as two by The Birkenhead Dock Company on the west side of the Mersey. A Royal Commission was appointed to consider the development of the docks and in 1853 recommended the formation of a new body to take over responsibility for all the Mersey docks. In 1857, an Act of Parliament took away from Liverpool Borough the control of the docks and created the independent Mersey Docks and Harbour Board, an organisation which was neither nationalised, subsidised nor profit-making, but charged with the responsibility of managing the dock estate (it became the Mersey Docks and Harbour Company in 1972, and was bought by Peel Ports in 2005).

Busy scene at the Pier Head in the early 20th century, loading The Aquitania preparation for departure

New Trade Routes across the Globe

Sailing ships continued to transport emigrants to America in huge numbers, often in excess of 200,000 per year. In spite of the development of trade with other parts of the world, America remained the dominant partner. Liverpool's reliance on cotton from the Southern States to supply the cotton mills of Lancashire and beyond led to support for the Confederate cause. Nevertheless, the problems of supply of American cotton during the American Civil War caused new sources to be sought, in Egypt, India and the Far East, so that Liverpool could maintain its position as the world's market place for cotton.

The first steamship line from Liverpool to the Far East, the Ocean Steam Ship Company, known as the Blue Funnel Line, was founded by Alfred Holt. Liverpool was then pre-eminent on all oceans of the world. By 1873, the Pacific Steam Navigation Company was said to be the largest shipping company in the world and had its headquarters in Liverpool. Liverpool companies which traded with Africa, notably Elder Dempster (commenced 1868), had secured Britain's largest share of the West African trade.

A significant addition to the trade routes came with the Australian Gold Rush of the 1850s. A large number of new shipping lines mostly using sailing clippers, sprang up to meet the demand for speedy passages to Australia. Many of these lines were subsequently adapted to serve triangular routes, incorporating visits to San Francisco or the Far East. By 1850, Liverpool's export trade was double that of London and more than half that of the whole nation. More overseas trade was carried out here than in any other city in the world and this exemplifies Liverpool's global trading connections and culture.

© National Trust

View across Albert Dock from east with dockers on the quayside

The Early Twentieth Century Zenith

At the beginning of the 20th century, Liverpool was confident in its claim to be 'The Second City of the Empire'. The value of its imports and exports exceeded the combined value of those from Bristol, Manchester, Southampton and Hull and manufacturing industries were being established in and around the city to take advantage of the proximity of the docks. The docks themselves continued to grow and adapt to meet the needs of the new industries.

In celebration of Liverpool's 700th Anniversary in 1907, Ramsey Muir compiled his comprehensive, if personal, *History of Liverpool*, and in it he proclaimed that the dock system at that time had no rival anywhere in the world:
'For seven and a quarter miles, on the Lancashire side of the river alone the monumental granite, quarried from the board's own quarries in Scotland, front the river in a vast sea wall as solid and enduring as the Pyramids, the most stupendous work of its kind that the will and power of man has ever created...It is here, besides the docks, that the citizens of Liverpool can best feel the opulent romance of the city, and the miracle of transformation which has been wrought since the not distant days when, where the docks now stand, the untainted tides of the Mersey raced past a cluster of mud hovels amid fields and untilled pastures.'

In keeping with this mood of pride in the fruits of enterprise, the city's commercial district was booming, with trade connections across the whole world. Liverpool had become a centre for underwriting, exchanges, insurance and banking, mostly under the control of Liverpool shipowners. In a staggering display of self-confidence, the Mersey Docks and Harbour Board, the Cunard Steamship Company and the Royal Liver Insurance Company, with municipal support, redefined the appearance of the Pier Head by building three new showpiece buildings on the site of George's Dock, looking assertively outwards to the river and the world.

Post World War I

A downturn in the city's economy and the fortunes of the docks began after the First World War and inevitably the inequitable casual labour system used in the vast majority of the docks led to great unemployment. Yet some investment

Anglican Cathedral

continued in both the docks and the city. Gladstone Dock, with a water area of 52 acres and one of the largest graving docks in Europe at the time, was opened in 1927. In the city, new temples to commerce were constructed, such as the monumental Martins Bank Building and India Buildings. These almost rivalled the great 20th-century temples to God – Giles Gilbert Scott's Anglican Cathedral (1903-1986), the last great Gothic cathedral in the world; Sir Edwin Lutyens' abandoned Catholic Cathedral (1933-40), which was to have had the widest dome in the world; and Sir Frederick Gibberd's completed Metropolitan (Catholic) Cathedral (1962-7), a buttressed geometric drum, which rises above Lutyens' partially completed crypt and is known locally as 'Paddy's Wigwam'. The City Council also continued to make improvements, assisting in the construction of the East Lancashire Road from Liverpool to Manchester, and the Mersey Queensway Tunnel, which opened in 1934.

World War II

Liverpool suffered more from enemy bombing during World War II than any other provincial city, because of its docks and their strategic value to the nation in importing food and other supplies. There were 15,000 blitzed sites in Liverpool. The docks were heavily damaged, as were adjacent areas, including the Custom House, India Buildings, the Corn Exchange and the Central Library and Museum. It was not only Liverpool itself that suffered; there were severe losses at sea to Liverpool-owned ships and other ships bound to and from the port. Nevertheless, over 1,000 convoys entered Liverpool during the war, bringing vital supplies of food, raw materials and men.

The Battle of the Atlantic was the longest running campaign of the war. The first encounter, the sinking of the SS Athenia bound for Canada from Liverpool, occurred within 24 hours of the outbreak of hostilities. The last encounter, the loss of the British freighter Avondale Park and a Norwegian minesweeper, took place more than six years and eight months later.

Post War Rebuilding

It was a massive challenge to repair the damage to the docks and the city caused during the war. The Mersey Docks and Harbour Board modernised some of the docks and improved the approaches from the sea. Liverpool City Council and private landowners began the task of repairing and rebuilding structures where necessary, but there are still vacant sites in the city which have not been redeveloped since wartime bombing.

Bomb damage May 1941 looking south from Castle Street to Custom House

© John 'Hoppy' Hopkins

Urban Regeneration

The 1950s and 60s was a period of great cultural creativity in the city. The phenomenal success of the Beatles and Merseybeat had an impact far beyond the city's boundaries but was much influenced by Liverpool's strong links with America. The period of economic respite in the 1960s was followed by increasingly severe difficulties during subsequent decades. Britain's retreat from Empire and the growing importance of European trade meant that Liverpool found itself on the wrong side of the country to take advantage of that trade. Containerisation, combined with the trend towards larger vessels, increased the speed of cargo handling, and rendered obsolete the wharves and warehouses of the historic docks.

In 1972, the South Docks, including Albert Dock were closed to commercial traffic and in 1974 they became tidal, leading to heavy siltation. The Merseyside Development Corporation was formed in 1981, and became operationally involved in the regeneration of the Mersey waterfront. Its remit included the revitalisation of these docks as part of the overall restoration of the South Docks Water Regime, together with the refurbishment of the majestic Hartley warehouses at Albert and Wapping Docks (and later Waterloo Warehouse). The dredging of the docks and the installation of new dock gates at Canning facilitated the Tall Ships spectaculars, first held in 1984, as well as the immensely popular Mersey River Festivals. Further upstream, the new river entrance lock at Brunswick facilitated the opening of the Liverpool Marina. This marked the beginning of Liverpool's urban regeneration through its maritime heritage.

Environmental and economic regeneration has continued through the beginning of the 21st century due in part to European Union support, resulting in over £1.3 billion of public sector money (European and national) spent on economic development in the conurbation. Liverpool City Council, a range of public sector organisations and the private sector have formed partnerships to facilitate the transformation of the city centre and the waterfront, in many cases re-using the historic buildings and docks.

Although many deep seated problems remain, Liverpool's economy has enjoyed a decade of solid achievement and for the first time in seventy years, the city's population is beginning to rise. The port is handling more tonnage of goods than ever before and in 2013 Peel Ports began the construction of Liverpool 2, a new 854 metre quay wall in the river, which will double the current container capacity of the Port of Liverpool and enable the biggest ships to visit, without having to enter the dock system. Following the completion of Grosvenor's Liverpool One retail-led development in 2008, the city centre's retail ranking has moved from 29th in the national league table, to number five, thus restoring its pre-war status. The universities are attracting record numbers of Chinese and other overseas students, giving the city centre a new cosmopolitan air.

Tall Ships in the Mersey

Kings Dock Convention Centre and Arena

Liverpool One

More than three decades of waterfront regeneration have created a series of attractions, with much improved inter-linked public spaces at the Pier Head and further south. Ambitious, though controversial, plans from Peel Holdings for its £5bn Liverpool Waters development have the potential to extend the waterfront regeneration and public access to the waterfront north from the Pier Head.

Liverpool's World Heritage Site is now at the heart of a vibrant city centre which is increasingly a destination for cultural tourists. The tourism and conference sectors have grown from virtually nothing over the last three decades to become major employers. In a survey by Impacts08 in 2008, 74% of visitors said that the WHS was an important factor in influencing their visit to the city. In January 2014, the travel bible *Rough Guide* named Liverpool the top UK city and third in the world for people to visit. It has also risen swiftly in the international league tables as a conference destination with the flexibility offered by the arena and convention centre at Kings Dock which opened in 2008. Despite the property recession, many new hotels have opened, four occupying historic buildings in the World Heritage Site: at Stanley Dock, Albion House, the Royal Insurance Building and the former Municipal Annex (originally Liverpool Conservative Club). The national perception of Liverpool has been transformed, as the success of the European Capital of Culture in 2008 has brought wider knowledge of the city's culture, art and architecture as well as the long-standing attractions of football, Beatles and the Grand National. The European Capital of Culture made people realise that Liverpool is a cultured city: UNESCO's inscription of Liverpool as a World Heritage Site confirms that Liverpool is a historic city of global significance.

The QE2 docked in Liverpool's new cruise liner terminal in 2007

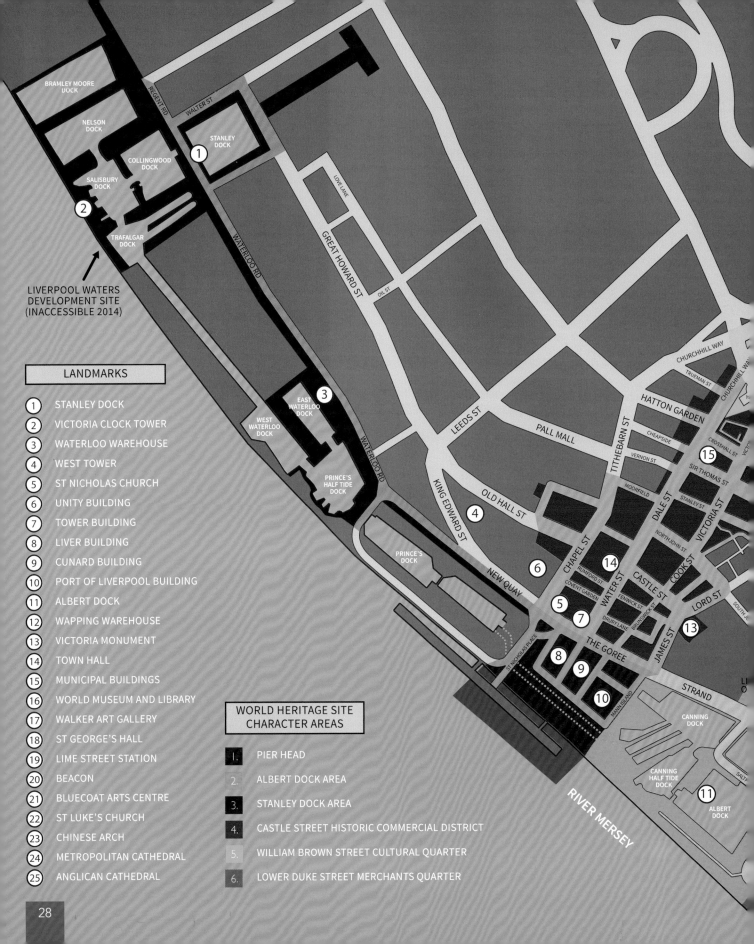

LIVERPOOL WATERS
DEVELOPMENT SITE
(INACCESSIBLE 2014)

LANDMARKS

1. STANLEY DOCK
2. VICTORIA CLOCK TOWER
3. WATERLOO WAREHOUSE
4. WEST TOWER
5. ST NICHOLAS CHURCH
6. UNITY BUILDING
7. TOWER BUILDING
8. LIVER BUILDING
9. CUNARD BUILDING
10. PORT OF LIVERPOOL BUILDING
11. ALBERT DOCK
12. WAPPING WAREHOUSE
13. VICTORIA MONUMENT
14. TOWN HALL
15. MUNICIPAL BUILDINGS
16. WORLD MUSEUM AND LIBRARY
17. WALKER ART GALLERY
18. ST GEORGE'S HALL
19. LIME STREET STATION
20. BEACON
21. BLUECOAT ARTS CENTRE
22. ST LUKE'S CHURCH
23. CHINESE ARCH
24. METROPOLITAN CATHEDRAL
25. ANGLICAN CATHEDRAL

WORLD HERITAGE SITE CHARACTER AREAS

1. PIER HEAD
2. ALBERT DOCK AREA
3. STANLEY DOCK AREA
4. CASTLE STREET HISTORIC COMMERCIAL DISTRICT
5. WILLIAM BROWN STREET CULTURAL QUARTER
6. LOWER DUKE STREET MERCHANTS QUARTER

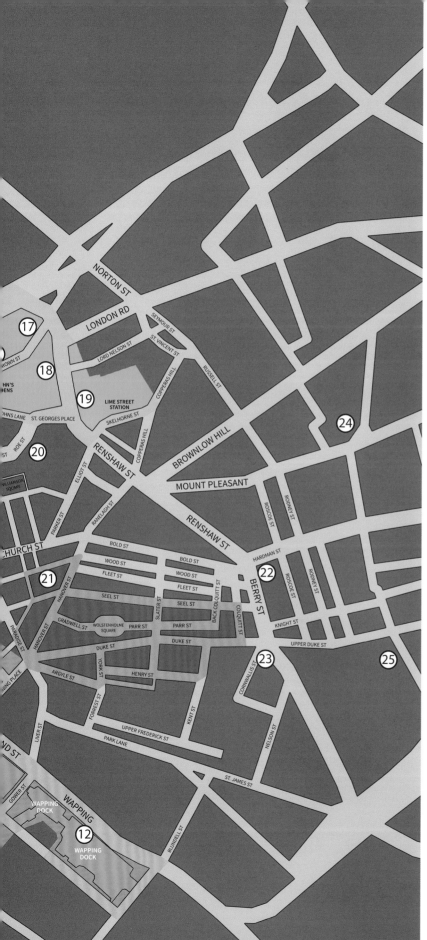

The World Heritage Site: Its Boundary, Six Areas and a Buffer Zone

The irregular shape of Liverpool's World Heritage Site seems unfathomable to many on first sight, but the boundary was drawn after careful consideration to ensure that it meets UNESCO's tests of 'outstanding universal value, authenticity and integrity'. The objective was to include all those parts of the historic city which relate to its function as a commercial port city. Like all cities, Liverpool had distinct quarters, where different activities took place and are reflected in the varied building types which remain. The World Heritage Site is therefore divided into six areas of distinctive townscape character which tell the story of those activities. This eases description, enables better understanding of how the port city worked and helps generate more effective planning guidance for each of the areas:

1. Pier Head - the centre of the historic waterfront where the city centre meets the River Mersey

2. Albert Dock Conservation Area - a system of historic docks and warehouses to the south of the Pier Head, stretching from the river to the edge of the modern Liverpool One shopping centre

3. Stanley Dock Conservation Area - another group of historic docks and maritime buildings, to the north of the Pier Head and linked to the Leeds and Liverpool Canal

4. Castle Street Historic Commercial District - the commercial core of buildings from the 18th century onwards, based around the medieval street pattern

5. William Brown Street Cultural Quarter - an ensemble of 19th century (mostly cultural) buildings, demonstrating the city's interest in cultural values as well as commercial gain

6. Lower Duke Street Merchants Quarter – a district of early merchant's houses and warehouses, which developed from the early 18th century after infilling of the tidal Pool of Liverpool and the construction of Old Dock

A Buffer Zone has been designated round the World Heritage Site, as recommended by UNESCO to give an added layer of protection to the property. It includes the immediate setting, and landmarks such as the two cathedrals from where excellent views over the World Heritage Site can be enjoyed.

PIER HEAD

View of Pier Head from the Museum of Liverpool with the Canal Link, Mersey Ferry Terminal and a liner at the Cruise Line Terminal

© John Hinchliffe

George's Dock circa 1907, with roads across it awaiting development of the two northern plots

The trio of monumental buildings, recently nicknamed 'The Three Graces', is a testament to Liverpool's pre-eminence in global trade in the early years of the 20th century. The buildings occupy the site of the former George's Dock, constructed in 1771, which had become obsolete by the 1890s. These great buildings, erected for the Mersey Docks and Harbour Board, the Royal Liver Friendly Society and the Cunard Steamship Company, were the result of a long-cherished vision to enhance the city's maritime gateway. Commercially driven, stridently individual in character and self-advertising in intent, they give Liverpool its unforgettable image as a port city.

HISTORY

The Mersey Docks and Harbour Board, which assumed control of the dock estate from Liverpool Corporation in 1857 by government decree, considered filling in the George's Dock as early as 1871. But its priorities were the commercial prosperity of the port, and not municipal improvements. They were therefore wary when the Corporation first suggested that the dock be used for new building sites and a waterfront public space. Yet the Board was tempted by the idea of building its own head offices on part of the site; and when the Corporation made a good offer for the dock, they agreed, reserving a portion of land for their own use. The plan involved extending the three existing streets that ran down to the dockside – Water Street, Brunswick Street and James Street – across the dock in the form of viaducts, leaving large development plots for new buildings. A great waterfront piazza was to be created in front of the buildings which would cater for the bustling interchange of ocean liners, cross-river ferries, trams and trains.

To select a designer for its new offices, the Board held a competition, which was won by local architects Briggs Wolstenholme and Thornley with a grand Neo-Baroque design. Immediately following the appointment in August 1901, the Board sent the selected architect Frank Briggs to New York to look at how American offices were constructed and equipped. Returning fresh with new ideas, he refined the scheme, and added the central dome in response to criticisms that the building was not sufficiently eye-catching. Construction commenced in March 1903 and the new offices opened in 1907 to great acclaim.

Development of the other two sites took longer. It was not until June 1906 that a serious purchaser emerged for the northern site in the form of the Royal Liver Friendly Society, which wished to move from its crowded premises in the eastern suburbs. Negotiations for the purchase had been carried out by the architect Aubrey Thomas, and there was consternation when the plans were revealed. Most vociferous in opposition was the Mersey Docks and Harbour Board, which considered that the Royal Liver's offices would completely spoil the effect of their own landmark building. The local press reported on the controversy, describing it as one of the chief topics of conversation in the city and its Council Chamber over several months.

The central site took even longer to develop. Some regarded it as an ideal site for public baths, others favoured new offices for the city's tramway system. A further scheme envisaged a new Custom House on the site. In the end none of these came to fruition, and when in 1913 the Cunard Steamship Company announced its intention to build head offices in Liverpool, the last building block fell into place.

Fifteen years later, another major building joined the 'Three Graces' at the Pier Head. This was the Ventilation and Control Station for the Mersey Road Tunnel, one of a number of fine buildings erected on both sides of the river in connection with this great engineering enterprise.

The waterfront piazza has continuously evolved since it was reclaimed from the river in 1771. Initially it served as quaysides and marshalling yards for the George's Dock, and from 1829 it housed public baths, filled with sea water from the river. It has also acted as a point of embarkation and arrival for passenger vessels, from cross-river ferries to transatlantic liners; and in the early 20th century it was a chaotic space colonised by trams and cluttered with temporary shelters. In 2008 it was completely re-paved, incorporating a waterway link between the Leeds and Liverpool Canal and the Albert Dock. The Pier Head is one of the largest public spaces in the city centre, and provides a venue for major public gatherings. Its cultural significance is celebrated by a diversity of statuary and memorials, mostly to those who have lost their lives at sea.

One of many stained glass windows in the Port of Liverpool Building.
This one proclaiming the trading place of the Mersey Docks and
Harbour Board: Business in Great Waters

HIGHLIGHTS

Port of Liverpool Building (1903-07)

This proud building in the English Baroque style is faced in Portland stone, hung from a steel frame. Its basement walls, set within the dock, were waterproofed against the surge of seawater which entered the viaducts below the flanking streets. It is a four square block with corner turrets surmounted by cupolas, and in the centre is the great dome. Originally there was a mansard roof with an attic lit by dormers, but this was destroyed in the war and replaced by the present floor built above the cornice.

The interior, which is open to the public (by restricted permission of the owners), is no less impressive. Corridors from the main river entrance and from two of the corners lead to a central octagonal hall with galleries above. Below the dome are inscribed the poetic words of Psalm 107: 'They that go down to the Sea in Ships: that do business in great waters: These see the Works of the Lord: and his wonders in the deep'. Inside and out there is carving and decoration on maritime themes, including allegorical statues and bronze dolphins bearing globes with gilded continents. The lift cages are encrusted with sea horses and anchors, and the windows of the central hall and corridors are filled with stained glass depicting the coats of arms of the colonies and dominions of the British Empire. In the minds of all those who entered at the time of its opening in 1907, there was no doubt that the building stood as a symbol of commerce and the whole nation's imperial ambitions for the Port of Liverpool.

Port of Liverpool Building, built as the office of the Mersey Docks and Harbour Board

Royal Liver Building

Royal Liver Building (1908-11)

When constructed in 1908-11, this was the tallest and probably the most original office building in Britain. It was described as a skyscraper in the local press. Its architect, Aubrey Thomas, however, is something of an enigma. He was known at the time more for his cultivation of the business community than for advancing the cause of architecture, and none of his previous works, all in Liverpool, prefigure the startling design of the Liver Building. Its great scale and the complex stepping back of the upper storeys and towers could not have been achieved without the use of the new technology of ferro-concrete. Adopting the system patented by the French engineer François Hennebique, this allowed all the elements of construction – the floors, walls, arches, beams and columns – to act together, transferring the loads down to the foundations, and Thomas worked creatively with his engineer L G Mouchel to erect the gigantic building at astonishing speed. Each of the ten main storeys took an average of nineteen working days, and once the concrete was in place, it was possible to start the external wall construction on three different levels simultaneously. The demand for granite to face the building was supplied by quarries in Norway and Sweden as well as Scotland, and although the cladding is only a few inches thick, it gives the building a tremendous sense of weight and permanence.

Thomas's chief source for this extraordinary design must have been North America. There are echoes of Louis Sullivan's Auditorium Building of 1886-89 in Chicago in the varied bands of round headed windows and deeply recessed openings, while the concept of eye-catching towers as a device to give commercial buildings a memorable skyline had been pioneered in Manhattan in the first wave of skyscrapers. But the building's silhouette of cubic forms, spiced with a hint of eastern exoticism and Hawksmoor's London city churches is entirely unprecedented. No less astonishing are the gigantic liver birds, adopted by the Society as its emblem, which perch on top of the domes of the two towers with their wings outspread.

The building cost £650,000, more than twice as much as the Dock Offices, and was far larger than the Society needed. Yet for the Friendly Society, which had been founded sixty years earlier as a burials and thrift institution in a modest house in Vauxhall, the poorest area of the city, this stupendous new building was the best advertisement that it could have secured. It is a symbol of ambition, innovation and insurance.

Royal Liver Building under construction

Cunard Building

Cunard Building (1913-16)

By comparison with the Liver Building, Cunard's headquarters is a much quieter and more dignified design. It is in the style of a Renaissance palazzo, but just as with the other two buildings at the Pier Head, its architects were influenced by American practice. For the palazzo model had already been adapted by New York architects such as Mc Kim Mead and White for multi-storey buildings, and the Cunard Building looks more like a 5th Avenue apartment block than a Roman palace. The designer was Arthur J Davis of Mewes and Davis, who was responsible for the sumptuous Parisian-style interiors of the Cunard's flagship Aquitania. The detailed design, construction and fitting out was done by local architects Willink & Thicknesse. The structure is of reinforced concrete, clad in Portland stone.

As well as head offices, the building served as a passenger terminal, with graded accommodation as found on board ship. First class passengers had use of a lounge on the ground floor with a view of the river, while second and third class quarters were in the basements below. The larger Cunard ships were equipped to carry upwards of 2000 third-class passengers, coming from all parts of the Continent, as well as from Britain and Ireland, and virtually all would have passed through the building before embarking. The magnificently decorated public spaces were intended to evoke the character of the great Cunard ships, giving passengers a foretaste of the refinement and comfort they might expect to find on board. Today it stands as a symbol of the mass European emigration to the New World, of which Liverpool was the principal port of embarkation.

After the completion of the Pier Head project, the national architectural press deplored the lack of a uniform treatment, and asked why the Corporation had allowed three different architects, all creating buildings for office use, to produce designs representing separate phases in the post-classical tradition. Sir Charles Reilly, notable Professor of Architecture at the University of Liverpool at this time, called it 'one of the best, or worst, examples of excessive individualism in architecture'. Yet, these views on individualism and harmony no longer seem important to us today, and the contrasts enhance, rather than diminish our enjoyment of this memorable waterfront scene.

George's Dock Ventilation and Control Station (1932-34; reconstructed 1951-52)

Between the Port of Liverpool Building and the Strand is a fourth highlight. Rather than a Palace of Commerce, this is a Temple of Power, for it acts as a ventilation shaft and control station for the Mersey Road Tunnel. Designed by the architect Herbert J Rowse, with engineers Sir Basil Mott and J A Brodie, the building is in the Art Deco style, its streamlined form symbolising the age of the motor car. The dominant tower is flanked by offices, and at the centre are huge fans that expel the engine fumes from the tunnel below, replacing them with clean air. Relief sculptures by Edmund C Thompson and George C Capstick on the themes of Civil Engineering, Construction, Architecture and Decoration are found on the north and south facades, and on the west front is a figure with helmet and goggles, Speed - the Modern Mercury. The black basalt statues in niches are of Night and Day, symbols of the tunnel which never closes.

George's Dock Ventilation Tower and Central Station of the Mersey Road Tunnel

Basalt sculpture of 'Day' on west elevation of George's Dock Ventilation Tower

© English Heritage

Memorial to the Auxiliary Services of the Merchant navy

PUBLIC MONUMENTS AND SCULPTURE

The Pier Head piazza is rich in monuments and sculpture. The most evocative is the Memorial to All Heroes of Marine Engine Rooms, which is found at the north end just beyond the floating roadway. Sculpted by William Goscombe John, c.1916, it was conceived as a monument to the 32 engineers of the Titanic, who remained at the posts on the tragic night of 15 April 1912. The two pairs of engineers are not idealised, but portrayed with great naturalism, and it is one of the earliest monuments dedicated to the working man. The equestrian bronze Statue of Edward VII, erected in 1911 is also by Goscombe John, and is more typical of the period.

In front of the Royal Liver Building is the Memorial to Sir Alfred Lewis Jones, of 1913, the work of Sir George Frampton. Jones was a ship owner, and founded the Liverpool School of Tropical Medicine. It takes the form of a slender granite pedestal, at the top of which is a female figure representing Liverpool. She carries a model of a ship set upon a globe, Welcoming Commerce to the Port of Liverpool. The Memorial to the Merchant Navy, 1952 is dedicated to the 1,390 Merchant Navy seamen who lost their lives in World War II. It consists of a Portland stone platform with curved walls and a pair of globes, with sculpture by Herbert Tyson Smith.

© John Hinchliffe

Detail of engine room workers on Memorial to All Heroes of Marine Engine Rooms (The Titanic Memorial)

THE EMBARKATION, WATERLOO DOCKS LIVERPOOL

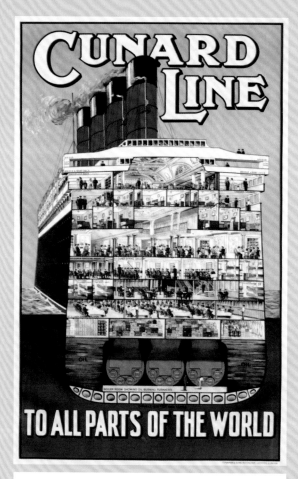

EMIGRATION

Between 1840 and 1914 almost 35 million Europeans emigrated to the New World, mostly seeking the promise of a better life. The scale of emigration grew with the multiplication in the number of ships capable of crossing the Atlantic in a reasonable time and the huge reduction in the cost of passage. In 1825 a ticket from Liverpool to America cost £20, but by 1863 it had fallen to £4.15s on a steamship and as little as £3 on a sailing ship. While several British ports including London, Bristol and Glasgow, operated transatlantic services, the majority of emigrants left from Liverpool, mostly heading for New York. Between 1860 and 1914, 4,750.000 passengers embarked at Liverpool out of a total of 5,500,000 leaving Great Britain. The majority came from western and northern Europe, particularly from Britain and Ireland, but towards the end of the 19th century some came from further afield.

To speed this vast movement of people, the Mersey Docks and Harbour Board built Riverside Station at Princes Dock which opened in 1895. It was reached by a long tunnel from Edge Hill to Waterloo Dock, where trains ran along the dock railway to the platforms at Princes Dock, giving direct access to the floating landing stage. It was said that many emigrants from Scandinavia and Germany would board trains at Hull and go directly to Liverpool where they embarked onto ships without setting foot on British soil. However, a majority would spend a night or more waiting to board their ship, and would be met by representatives of the shipping company and taken to lodgings. Thus Liverpool held poignant memories for many emigrants as their point of departure from Europe, and is a popular starting point for subsequent generations to trace their family roots.

Many passenger shipping lines had their headquarters in Liverpool, including White Star, Dominion, Cunard, Inman and Blue Funnel. Most early steamship companies declined to carry emigrants, but as competition increased, emigrants were actively recruited through agents across Europe. The Cunard Building erected at the Pier Head in 1914-16 was the ultimate expression of confidence in the future of the transatlantic service. Yet by the turn of the century Liverpool's share of the emigrant trade had begun to decline as emigrants increasingly came from south and east Europe. Other factors too conspired to slow down the rate of emigration to America. Restrictions on immigration imposed by the USA in 1926 and the two World Wars diminished Liverpool's role. During the inter-war period there was intense competition between the big European companies. Cunard made great efforts to retain its position as the leader in first class passenger transport, taking almost 42,000 passengers in that class in 1930, but it had moved its main port of embarkation to Southampton in 1921.

HERITAGE ACHIEVEMENTS SINCE INSCRIPTION

The Pier Head forcefully demonstrates Liverpool's cultural Renaissance since the inscription of the World Heritage Site. The centenaries of the Port of Liverpool Building and the Liver Building were celebrated in 2007 and 2011 respectively by full-scale restorations, with the Liver Building receiving an elegant glazed entrance on the river side to give shelter from the Atlantic gales. The Cunard Building, which will be 100 years old in 2016, is currently being acquired by Liverpool City Council for a return to its original use. Cruise passengers will check in at its spectacular booking hall before making their way to the cruise liner terminal alongside. The sculpture and memorials that populate the waterfront piazza were all conserved during the remodelling of the Pier Head and given a more dignified setting. The Memorial to All Heroes of Marine Engine Rooms was conserved in 2012, including the re-gilding of the flame and the sun, to commemorate the centenary of the tragic sinking of the Titanic on its maiden voyage.

IN NEED OF ATTENTION

There is one thing that is lacking – a commemorative plaque for the World Heritage Site, which every World Heritage Site is expected to display. The Pier Head would be the fitting place for this accolade, perhaps at the Cunard Building.

World Heritage Site emblem

Boys leaving Liverpool for a new life in Canada

During World War II millions of troops left for war on vessels sailing from Liverpool, and ship loads of American troops arrived bound for active service in Europe. In the early stages of the war, there was a mass evacuation of children to America and Canada, with liners carrying as many as 2,000 at a time. Some limited emigration picked up after the war, but competition from air travel increasingly reduced the numbers travelling by sea, and in 1967 even Cunard's passenger service came to an end.

Detail of Memorial to All Heroes of Marine Engine Rooms (The Titanic Memorial)

© John Hinchliffe

Pre-war view across Albert Dock from NW Corner, showing Clock Tower and Customs House beyond

Aerial view of Albert Dock in 1865, with Fosters Customs House and Liverpool Sailors' Home in top left corner

The Albert Dock Area is dominated by monumental dockside warehouses grouped around a system of historic docks. It was originally a hive of activity, alive with dockers, sailors, ships, horses and the produce of the world being lifted, lowered and carted around. The commercial activities in the area ceased in 1972 but it was re-invented as a new city quarter in the 1980s. Following the construction of Liverpool One, the Kings Arena and Conference centre, and the Museum of Liverpool from 2008, it has once again been integrated into the physical and social fabric of the city.

HISTORY

The creation of docks in this area was commenced in the early 18th century by infilling the Pool of Liverpool and reclaiming the tidal margins of the River Mersey. Until then, the Pool had formed a barrier which restricted the growth of the town southwards; but in 1709 the Corporation made the bold decision to fill it in, and appointed Thomas Steers to construct what became the world's first commercial enclosed wet dock. It opened in 1715 and subsequently became known as Old Dock. The main benefit of an enclosed dock was that once ships had entered the dock, they stayed at a continuous level to the quayside rather than rising and falling with the tide, and their goods could be loaded and unloaded with relative ease.

The success of this venture encouraged the Town Council to invest in further docks, gradually reclaiming land from the river in a westward direction. Canning Dock was constructed around 1737 as a dry, tidal dock. This was followed by Salthouse Dock in 1753, Canning Graving Docks in 1756, Duke's Dock in 1773 and Canning Half-tide Dock in 1844.

Albert Dock and its enclosing warehouses were built to the designs of Jesse Hartley, the Dock Engineer from 1824 to 1860, and was opened by Prince

Loading ship at Albert Dock

Opening of Albert Dock by Prince Albert in 1846

Aerial view of Albert Dock in 1980 with derelict warehouses and dock silted up.

Albert in 1846. Hartley engaged the assistance of the architect Philip Hardwick who had previously worked on the warehouses at Katharine's Dock in London and designed the famous Euston Arch which formed the entry to Euston Station. The Albert Dock warehouses were amongst the earliest to be fire-proofed, built of incombustible brick, stone and iron. Wapping Basin and Wapping Dock followed in 1855 with Wapping Warehouse, similar to those at Albert Dock being completed the following year.

The whole area was built to accommodate ships and for storing the goods which they brought in and took away. It operated successfully for decades, and was adapted continually to respond to changing demands and improved technology. However, as ships grew bigger and bulk transfer of commodities increased, these early docks and their warehouses became increasingly obsolete and their maintenance declined. The area suffered during WWII when it was damaged by enemy air-raids, and following further post-war decline the docks were finally closed in 1972. The Albert Dock warehouses were and still are the largest collection of Grade I listed buildings in England but their huge scale and poor condition were a massive conservation challenge. With the river gates left open and the docks themselves completely silted up, the future of the area was very much in doubt.

In 1981 the Merseyside Development Corporation was appointed to regenerate large areas of redundant dockland and worked with the Arrowcroft Group to restore the Albert and Wapping Dock warehouses and regenerate the area. The principles used in the conservation of the warehouses included respecting the 1846 plan, retaining the roof shape and colours, restoring original windows, and retaining all cast ironwork and artefacts.

The regeneration of the area was an immediate success and became the biggest free tourist attraction in the region, attracting over 4 million visitors per year. It was confirmed as an international model of heritage-led regeneration and marked the beginning of Liverpool's renewed confidence in using its maritime heritage as a source of civic pride. It is now home to many unique shops, restaurants, hotels, Tate Liverpool, The Beatles Story, the Museum of Liverpool, Merseyside Maritime Museum and apartments. Tall ships still visit, giving an authentic atmosphere and a reminder of how the dock would have been in its heyday.

The excavated remains of Old Dock are on display beneath Thomas Steers Way in Liverpool One.

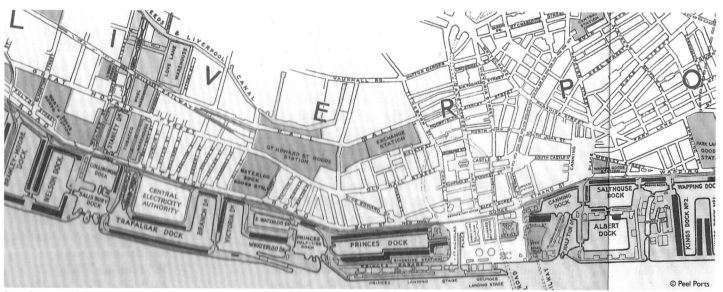

Plan of Liverpool Docks in 1950s

View across Albert Dock, framing Anglican Cathedral beyond in 2002

HIGHLIGHTS

Albert Dock Warehouses (1846) were the first publicly owned general warehouses on the Dock Estate. They were built exclusively for imported goods and were bonded: the goods received into the warehouses often stayed there for a considerable time and bonds in the goods could be bought at the time of import and sold at a profit; it was only when they were released from the warehouse that tax was paid. The robust character of the warehouses is the direct result of technological rigour and innovation. At Albert and Wapping, Hartley used well-established construction techniques adapted from textile mills, such as massive load-bearing external walls, fire-proof brick and stone floors, structural cast-iron columns and inverted iron Y-beams with wrought iron rods and brick barrel vaults. But he also introduced new solutions, such as the stressed-skin iron roof which can still be seen in the Dining Rooms on the fourth floor of the Maritime Museum. Hartley introduced some of the first hydraulic cargo-handling installations in the world for raising goods from the quaysides.

On the quayside, the warehouses have an open colonnade of cast iron Greek Doric columns, 3.8m in circumference and 4.5m high, except in the extension in the south west corner, where they are of granite. Arches rise from the ground level into the first floor, forming loading bays where hydraulic cranes were fixed for lifting goods out of the ships moored in the dock. The warehouses had recessed yards on the outer sides, where the goods were sent out, initially on horse drawn carts. The warehouses were all originally enclosed by a perimeter security wall, but it only survives on the west (river) side.

Rare surviving hydraulically powered crane at Albert Dock

Albert Dock Traffic Office

© John Hinchliffe

Dock Traffic Office (1846-7) was the visual and organisational focal point of the dock. It stands at the main roadway entrance to the dock and is where the comings and goings of ships and goods were regulated. Its huge portico of Tuscan columns, including the pediment is constructed entirely of cast iron and pushed the capabilities of that material to its limit. The four columns are 6m high, have a diameter of 1m at the base, and were cast in two halves and brazed together along their length. The architrave is 11.5m long and was made in a single casting, in the shape of a giant "U". Brazed onto the architrave is an iron cornice and pediment, consisting of seven separate castings. The building was restored along with the warehouses in the 1980s and initially re-opened as television studios, before being acquired by National Museums Liverpool for conversion into the dramatic entrance to the International Slavery Museum. Although slavery had been abolished in the British Empire at the time that Albert Dock was built, Canning Graving Docks (1765-8), where 18th century slave trading ships were repaired and fitted out, is only yards away to the north.

© English Heritage

Wapping Warehouse, converted to apartments in 1980s and Hydraulic Pumping Station to the right

Wapping Warehouse (1856) is another Hartley warehouse similar to those at Albert and Stanley Docks, in brick, iron and slate. The building was

originally 232 metres long, had 40 bays and was divided into five fireproof sections, but it has been reduced in length following damage suffered in the May Blitz of 1941. Its original length can be gauged from the partially redundant colonnade of iron columns on the quayside. Each section had a hydraulically powered lift and an open two-storey elliptical arch on the quayside. The original granite perimeter wall still stands on the east side and incorporates the stumps of the stanchions of the Liverpool Overhead Railway, which ceased operation in 1956.

Wapping Dock Hydraulic Tower (1856) stands at the south end of Wapping Warehouse. It supplied the hydraulic power for the lifting machinery in the warehouse. It is the most southerly of Hartley's 'defensive' line of pseudo historic 'castles' which guarded Liverpool's docks. It has a battered Cyclopean granite base (see Dock Construction, p.39), while the upper part is octagonal brickwork with rusticated stone quoins. The date 1856 is incised at the top of the east face.

DOCK STRUCTURES, ARTEFACTS AND FITTINGS

The authentic character of the Albert Dock area relies on the remarkable survival of smaller original or early dock structures, artefacts and fittings which are vital evidence of the operation of the docks. These include;

© English Heritage

The second Hydraulic Pumping Station at Albert Dock, now the Pumphouse Inn

Albert Dock Hydraulic Pumping Station (c.1870), south of Canning Half-Tide Dock (Pumphouse Inn) is not the original pumping station but a later replacement built when G F Lyster had become dock engineer. It has an elaborate mixture of brick, sandstone and terra-cotta and was probably designed by Arthur Berrington, the long-serving architectural draughtsman in the Dock Office.

(Half of) The Rennie Bridge at passage between Canning Dock and Canning Half-tide Dock

Dock Master's House at Albert Dock, now part of the Merseyside Maritime Museum

Swing Bridge (c.1845),

known as The 'Hartley Bridge', over the entrance to Canning Dock is a standard design of double leaf swing bridge adopted on many of the dock passages, brought to Liverpool by John Rennie for use at Princes Dock (opened 1821). It works as a pair of cantilevers when swung 'off' or when virtually unladen, but as a three-pin arch when loaded. It is the last survivor of its kind.

Swing Bridge (c.1846)

known as the 'Rennie Bridge', between Canning Dock and Canning Half Tide Dock is to the rear of the pumping station. It is the last survivor of the lightweight footbridges, which were essential for anyone who worked in the docks to cross water gaps. It is a double leaf bar-stayed design, built during the modernisation of Canning Half-tide Dock, possibly in 1845.

Pier Master's House or Dock Master's House (c.1846)

is the only one of a group of four 'Dock residences' at Albert/Canning Pier Head to have survived the Blitz. Houses such as this were built all over the Dock Estate from 1801 onwards to accommodate essential workers, and by 1846 there was a total of 40 of them, of which no others survive. The provision of accommodation was a valuable addition to a man's income, but carried the penalty of making their tenants more available in the middle of the night!

DOCK CONSTRUCTION

The river wall at Albert Dock at low tide

The river wall at Albert Dock, keeping the mighty River Mersey at bay

Cooperage Building at Albert Dock where barrels were made and repaired, now part of the Merseyside Maritime Museum

Cooperage, Perimeter Wall and Courtyard (c.1845)

is where the casks for the produce stored in the warehouses were repaired. The coopers were needed for opening and re-bunging casks in order that their contents could be sampled by Customs (or prospective purchasers). It is now part of the Merseyside Maritime Museum.

The reclamation of land and the construction of docks and river walls in the Pool and the soft ground of the tidal margins (where the tidal range is up to 10 metres twice a day) were major civil engineering achievements. The method of construction started by protecting the sites from the tide by driving cast iron and timber sheet piles or coffer-dams into the substrata which then usually formed part of the permanent structure.

With the construction of Old Dock, there was the problem not only of battling with the tides on the west side but also the waters from the upper reaches of the Pool, constantly fed by the stream from the Moss Lake to the east, which had

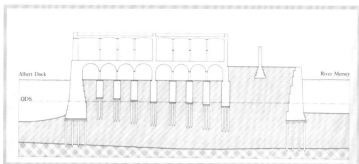
Cross section of piling for Albert Dock and river wall

to be diverted. Eventually the site of the dock was made reasonably watertight and then Steers had to dig down 18ft to the sandstone bedrock. It took five years and the walls were built in local common brick with sandstone copings. At Albert Dock, Jesse Hartley's river walls were built up in a series of corbelled layers to counteract the action of the swirling river. They still survive today and continue to keep the mighty River Mersey at bay. The Liverpool historian Ramsey Muir proclaimed them '...as solid and enduring as the Pyramids of Giza.'

The buildings and quay walls at Albert were mostly founded on a complex arrangement of timber piles and stone caps. In 1840, Hartley took a series of borings up to 52 feet deep to establish firm ground. In 1841 he was authorised to order three to four thousand beech or elm trees for piling. The circular section piles were lightly charred to help preserve them and this seems to have worked as the buildings still stand on the original timbers with minimal settlement. In 1842 an order for cast-iron sheet piles and connecting cramps was made. After securing the site, the north, south and west stacks of the warehouses were piled and capped beneath the basement columns and the external walls. The east warehouses were closer to the bedrock and so were built on inverted brick arches rather than piles.

The materials used for dock retaining walls also reflect improvements in technology. Old Dock was faced with small bricks with a sandstone coping, but the brick walls proved to be structurally inadequate when buffeted by large ships and had to be repaired on many occasions. In the next phase, such as Canning Dock and George's Dock the quay walls are constructed in large blocks of local sandstone. At Albert Dock and his other docks, Hartley used granite with his characteristic 'Cyclopean' coursing, randomly sized and shaped masonry, tightly jointed. The granite was imported from the Dock Board's own quarries in Scotland in its ship The Oak. The huge coping stones surmounting the dock retaining walls and forming the edge of the quayside are tied together by the use of small square locking stones.

WHAT THEY SAID

Prince Albert in his speech at the opening of the Albert Dock, 30th July 1846:
'I have heard of the greatness of Liverpool but the reality far surpasses the expectation':

James Picton, historian and architect (1805-89):
'The works for strength and durability are unsurpassable, but it is to be regretted that no attention whatsoever has been paid to beauty as well as strength. The enormous pile of warehouse is....simply a hideous pile of brickwork'.

Quentin Hughes in his seminal work *Seaport* (1964) was one of the first to laud the architectural qualities of the ensemble:
'We can appreciate the monumental solemnity of the design, stripped of the superfluous, a sound and economic solution to a set problem...Satisfaction is gained from appreciating the large areas of plain brickwork carefully

proportioned, the individual characteristics of the bricks subordinated to the monolithic appearance, the bold statement of iron columns, and the play of light on the reflecting water whose mirror dissolves the substance of reality into a shimmering phantasy'.

Diary of George Holt Esq, Shipowner (circa 1846)
'...walked round the new Albert Dock Warehouses - most lavish expense everywhere; the construction is for eternity, not time; it appears prodigally extravagant'.

HERITAGE ACHIEVEMENTS SINCE INSCRIPTION

Perhaps the greatest achievement has been the way that the Albert Dock has been harmoniously integrated into the surrounding city by the effective planning of new development around it:

Liverpool One

Prior to the construction of the Liverpool One development, Albert Dock seemed isolated and remote from the city centre. While the busy road of The Strand remains a partial barrier, the layout of Liverpool One and in particular the linking pedestrian route of Thomas Steers Way have dramatically re-connected Albert Dock with the city. This provides a direct practical route and visual framing of Albert Dock and seems to physically draw pedestrians towards it. Within Liverpool One, the cultural heritage has been revealed to make it much more than a modern retail and leisure destination:

- the Old Dock has been partially excavated and presented, with a viewing hole outside the north west corner of John Lewis store, and a line of fountains and contrasting paving above its northern quay. The below-ground attraction can be visited, see: http://www.liverpoolmuseums.org.uk/maritime/visit/old_dock_tours.aspx
- the importance of the tides is celebrated by the circular Moon Pool at the west end of Thomas Steers Way
- the route of the Pool of Liverpool is recalled in the paving along Thomas Steers Way and the early revetments and vegetation is recalled in the edges of the Moon Pool
- the underlying red sandstone bedrock is continued up to retain the high ground of the new Chavasse Park which also emphasises the dominating position of the former Liverpool Castle
- the role of Thomas Hutchinson, who lived on the site in the mid-18th century is celebrated in engravings in the paving along Thomas Steers Way. He was the world's first permanent dock master who took readings of every high tide, twice a day for 30 years and his research is still used to predict the time of tides
- the pre-existing historic street pattern has been re-established to ensure that the new development blends seamlessly with the surrounding historic city
- framed views of historic landmarks outside the site have been created, focussing on such structures as the Albert Dock, the Anglican Cathedral, the gilt dome of the Royal Insurance Building and the cupola of The Bluecoat.
- the few surviving historic structures on the site have been restored, notably the world's first American Consulate in Paradise Street and the two 18th century warehouses in College Lane
- the gates from the former Liverpool Sailors' Home have been rescued from their displaced location of 50 years in Sandwell (near Birmingham) and re-instated as close as possible to their original location in Paradise Street, forming a gateway to the development

Framed view of Albert Dock from Liverpool One looking down Thomas Steers Way

To the north, Albert Dock is now better connected to the Pier Head by three co-ordinated new developments on Mann Island:

Museum of Liverpool

The Museum of Liverpool, designed by Danish architects 3XN, was opened in 2011 and is widely recognised as an exciting contemporary addition to Liverpool's waterfront. It provides a sense of enclosure at the south end of the massive piazza and was designed to work with the new canal and basin, extending the public realm into and through the building. The external steps leading to the first floor provide a higher vantage point, complemented by the massive windows to north and south that give panoramic views of the surrounding area so that the city itself becomes part of the museum exhibit. Perhaps as important as its visual contribution as a building, the museum is a major attraction which brings people to the waterfront and tells the story of the City of Liverpool, including its people and the life of the port. It is therefore vital in transmitting the basis for Liverpool's inscription as a World Heritage Site.

Mann Island Development

The Mann Island Development, designed by Broadway Malyan, consists of three contemporary buildings, two containing apartments and public uses and the one nearest the Strand containing offices. Deliberately designed as three blocks rather than as a continuation of the Three Graces, its black geometric shapes and its location between the Albert Dock and the Pier Head reflect the nature of the dock water bodies rather than competing with their historic neighbours. The forms of the buildings and their composition were informed by analysing the important views from the south across Canning Dock, where they create dynamic, framed and sliced views of the Pier Head Group. The UNESCO/ICOMOS Mission to Liverpool in 2006 endorsed the design of the buildings prior to the grant of planning approval.

Leeds and Liverpool Canal Link

With the closure of Georges Dock at the end of the 19th century, the dock system to the south of the Pier Head was severed from the dock system to the north. The Leeds and Liverpool Canal link was completed by the Canal and Rivers Trust in 2009 to re-establish that connection and to enable barges to travel from the main canal system, through Stanley Dock and the Pier Head to a new berth in Salthouse Dock.

IN NEED OF ATTENTION

Canning Graving Docks

All principal buildings and structures within the Albert Dock Area are now in reasonable condition and contribute positively to the experience of visiting the area. The quayside of Canning Graving Docks is a highly atmospheric location, rich in maritime artefacts such as the propellor of the Lusitania, and hand-operated "gate engines" bearing the name Coalbrookdale Foundry, Liverpool. Regrettably, the area is currently fenced off due to concerns about public safety in the vicinity of the dry docks. National Museums Liverpool, the owners of the site, has prepared a proposal to make it accessible, but funding is not currently available.

View of Pier Head Group, framed by Mann Island Development

View of Princes Dock and St. Nicholas Church looking south from Princes Half Tide Dock circa 1890

View of Stanley Dock from Collingwood Dock in WG Herdman's "Modern Liverpool" (1864). NB The tower of the Hydraulic Pumping Station shown is that of the South Pumping Station, demolished to make way for the Tobacco Warehouse

The Stanley Dock area consists of two separate groups of historic docks linked by a long stretch of the dock boundary wall. The southern group consists of the Princes Half Tide Dock and the West Waterloo Dock, with its massive grain warehouse. Further north is the complex of five interlinked docks, which includes the Stanley Dock and the Salisbury Dock, as well as a section of the Leeds and Liverpool Canal. The area is characterised by robust dock walls and port-related structures, huge warehouses, and smaller-scale quayside artefacts. Ground surfacing in stone flags and granite setts, crisscrossed by rail tracks survive in many areas, creating a distinctive and dramatic urban landscape.

HISTORY

Following the development of Liverpool's enclosed dock system in the late 18th century, the construction of the Princes Dock, north of the Pier Head, marked the first substantial increase in the size of the docks. Although permission was granted by Act of Parliament in 1800, a shortage of funds, problems with land assembly and restrictions imposed by the Napoleonic Wars meant that work did not commence until 1810. Completed in 1821 by the Dock Engineer John Foster, it remained the largest dock in Liverpool until 1832, and was the flagship for Liverpool's trade with North America for both imported cotton and movement of people. Princes Dock was the first in Liverpool to be protected by a dock boundary wall.

Clarence Graving Docks

The next phase of the Central Docks was developed by Foster's successor Jesse Hartley who more than doubled the extent of the docks between 1824 and 1860. Rapid expansion was the result of huge growth in the textile industry and the opening of markets in India and China following the end of the East India Company's monopolies, and in South America. Hartley first built the Clarence Dock and Clarence Graving Dock some distance north of the Princes Dock, which opened in 1830. Clarence specialised in steamships and was sited away from the existing docks to reduce the fire risk to other vessels. Next came three interlinked docks – Waterloo, Victoria and Trafalgar – the first examples of spine and branch docks, with access from the dock network to north and south. They were sited between the Princes Dock and the Clarence Dock, and were completed by 1836. With the construction of these docks the boundary wall was extended to restrict access.

dock comprised two basins, of which the East Waterloo Dock was the grain dock, equipped with three large warehouses, only one of which now survives.

At the end of the century Stanley Dock, with its great bonded warehouses, was also radically changed. The principal commodity being stored in the warehouses was tobacco, but in order to improve operations, it was decided to make it a specialised tobacco dock with a new purpose-built warehouse. In 1898 half the dock basin was infilled, and construction of the gigantic Stanley Dock Tobacco Warehouse was commenced. When it opened in 1901, with its 1.3 million square feet of floor space, capable of holding 70,000 hogsheads of tobacco, it was the world's largest warehouse, and was for many years the Dock Board's most profitable building.

Extension of the Leeds and Liverpool Canal into the dock system by Jesse Hartley 1848

© English Heritage

Opening barrels of tobacco for sampling on the top floor of Tobacco Warehouse at Stanley Dock

© Peel Ports

Following the Dock Act of 1844, work began on a total of seven new docks for Liverpool. Five of these were planned and built by Hartley as a single construction programme. They are the Salisbury, Collingwood, Stanley, Nelson and Bramley-Moore Docks, and they were opened on 4 August 1848. As with the 1830s docks they formed an interlinked system, the Salisbury Dock forming the link to the river, with locks connecting to the other water bodies. Only Stanley Dock, which was linked to the Leeds and Liverpool Canal for onward transport of goods, was excavated from dry land; all the others were built out into the river as the earlier central docks had been. Stanley Dock was also the only one to be equipped with multi-storey warehouses of the type that Hartley had already built at the Albert Dock, and also benefitted from its connection to the Yorkshire and Lancashire Railway which opened up markets further afield.

Later in the 19th century, alterations were made to some of the Central Docks. The Princes Basin was modernised and rebuilt around 1868 by G F Lyster, Hartley's successor, as a half tide dock, with a river entrance and locks modelled on Hartley's design for Salisbury Dock. Lyster also remodelled the Waterloo Dock at the same time. The impetus for this was the repeal of the Corn Laws, which created the opportunity to import grain from North America, using the Waterloo Dock as a specialist bulk grain dock, the first in the world. The new

In the 20th century, as the size of ships increased and quicker turnaround times were required, the central docks became inadequate. In 1929 a programme of modernisation was begun, which ultimately led to the infilling of the Clarence Dock, Clarence Half Tide Dock and Victoria Dock. The Trafalgar Dock was reconstructed as a long narrow basin running parallel with the river wall, incorporating the Clarence Gridiron Dock Basin which provided access to the Clarence Graving Docks. The south end of this dock had a passage through to West Waterloo Dock. Today only the Graving Docks and the north end of the remodelled Trafalgar Dock remain, with the remainder having been infilled. A narrow waterway has been created linking the Salisbury Dock with the Princes Dock, and thence on to the Albert Dock as an extension of the Leeds and Liverpool Canal.

The impact of these changes on the authenticity of this central group of docks is the reason why they are not included in the World Heritage Site (although they are within the Buffer Zone). Likewise the Princes Dock was significantly altered in the 20th century and is excluded. The Princes Half Tide Dock and the East Waterloo Dock, however, remain largely unaltered since 1868, and are included in the World Heritage Site; as are the Clarence Graving Docks and the remarkable and well-preserved complex of five docks dating from 1848.

The 'Great Dock Wall of Liverpool', at Sandon Dock

HIGHLIGHTS

Dock Boundary Wall (1816-48) runs from the southern end of Princes Dock along the dock road as far as Huskisson Dock, a length of 2.75 km. It was built over a period of more than 30 years by different dock engineers. It is generally 5.5m high and is punctuated by a series of gateways leading into the various docks. Originally the wall ran right around each dock or group of docks, but now it survives only on the east side. The purpose of the wall was to control access into and out of the docks so as to prevent theft and smuggling of goods, and it effectively made the docks into a stronghold.

The earliest section was at Princes Dock, built 1816-21 by John Foster. It is of brick with stone copings and had monumental gateways in the classical style, only one of which survives. The next phase was built further north by Hartley to enclose his group of 1830s docks, and was completed by 1841. He continued Foster's style, using brick with stone copings and gateways, of which four survive. In the 1840s Hartley built the connecting link between Princes Dock and Waterloo Dock. Here again brick was used, although the four gateways are in granite adopting the style that Hartley used for his last phase.

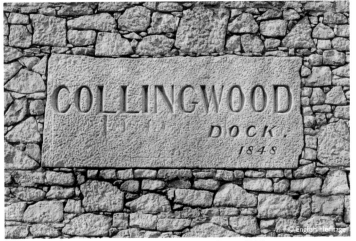

Granite name Plaque of Collingwood Dock in the Dock Security Wall

The final section of the wall enclosed the group of five docks which opened in 1848, and ran on further north as far as the Huskisson Dock. Here, instead of brick Hartley employed the 'Cyclopean' granite style of construction that he used in the dock retaining walls, with rounded copings. Set into the wall at intervals are granite plaques bearing the name of each dock and the date of construction, 1848. The gateways have double entrances with round tapering towers as gate piers. The central round tower functioned as an office for the dock policeman who controlled access. Timber gates, of which a few survive, slide out on rollers from slits in the gate piers.

The wall incorporates cast iron stanchions at intervals. These were inserted to support the Liverpool Overhead Railway, designed by James Greathead and Sir Douglas Fox for the Mersey Docks and Harbour Board in 1888. A number of cast iron drinking fountains are also recessed into the wall. These were installed in 1859 in an attempt to keep the dock workers out of the pubs. The dock wall, which originally stretched for five miles north and south of the city centre, is one of the defining features of the dock estate. With the almost complete removal of the wall in the historic south docks, the townscape impact of this fortress-like feature can now only be appreciated in the central docks.

Waterloo Warehouse, converted to apartments in 1980s

East Waterloo Dock (1834, reconstructed 1868) Hartley's original Waterloo Dock, one of three that he built as an interlinked system in the 1830s, was reconstructed by Lyster in 1868. The original rectangular dock had its short end facing the river, but Lyster converted it into two docks orientated north-south. The West Waterloo Dock provided berths for medium-sized ocean-going vessels, while the East Waterloo Dock became a specialist grain dock with three massive grain warehouses built on the quaysides. Only the warehouse on the east quayside remains, the north block having been destroyed in the bombing of 1941 and west block was demolished to create a short-lived container terminal at West Waterloo Dock in 1969.

The surviving grain warehouse is 43 bays long, divided into six sections by full height loading bays, with two hoist towers of an additional two storeys. It is built of brick with a colonnade of stone arches along the quayside. The basement and mezzanine levels held machinery and conveyor belts, which were operated throughout all three warehouses by a single hydraulically-driven system, placed in a separate engine house. The hydraulic system also operated three moveable bridges, ten ships capstans and 24 gate engines. The design was regarded at the time by James Picton, the Liverpool architect and historian, as 'a great improvement on the massive ugliness of the Albert Warehouses'.

Victoria Clock Tower at Salisbury Dock in 2002,
prior to demolition of single storey extensions

Victoria Clock Tower (1848)

Victoria Clock Tower (1848) stands on an island at the entrance to the Salisbury Dock, which provided access to the group of docks that opened in 1848. Hartley's innovative arrangement of a double entrance with an additional barge lock was given prominence by the construction of the spectacular tower. This six sided clock and bell tower is built of granite, and stands on the central island between the two sets of locks. It was designed to aid navigation, marking the time for seamen and ringing out the high tide and warnings in times of poor visibility. It contained a Pier Master's flat. Just to the south of the tower, built on the sea wall, is the Dock Master's Office, a robust building of granite with a machicolated parapet and crenellations like the bastion of a castle, which also dates from 1848.

Hydraulic Engine House, Bramley-Moore Dock (1884)

Hydraulic Engine House, Bramley-Moore Dock (1884) stands to the north east of the Bramley-Moore Dock and consists of a brick engine house and accumulator tower with a truncated octagonal chimney. Attached to the rear are remains of the overhead coal railway that led to the quaysides of the Bramley-Moore Dock. The building was erected in 1884 by Lyster to provide hydraulic power for the operation of the lock gates, capstans and swing bridges for some of the docks. Its design is not as fanciful as those at Stanley Dock or Birkenhead Docks, but it is a landmark within the dockland.

Aerial View of Stanley Dock, circa 2002

Stanley Dock

Stanley Dock (opened along with the other four docks on 4 August 1848) was linked to the Leeds and Liverpool Canal for transport of low-cost bulky goods such as coal from Lancashire and Yorkshire, and for imported cotton on its way to the Lancashire mill towns. Between 1852 and 1855 Hartley built two large warehouses to the north and south of the dock basin, similar to those he had already constructed at the Albert Dock in 1846. These differ from the Albert and Wapping Dock warehouses in that the external walls are built entirely of brick, apart from a granite plinth and a sandstone band on the South Warehouse only. The north warehouse retains its colonnade of cast iron columns along the edge of the quayside, but at the south warehouse the elliptical arches were infilled with brick when the Tobacco Warehouse was erected. The north warehouse was damaged in wartime bombing and ceased use altogether in 1985; but it was restored and re-opened as a hotel in 2014. Its eastern end was replaced by a single storey addition in 1953 for use as storage for rum which is now in use as a conference centre. Items of hydraulic machinery, mostly dating from around 1900, survive in both warehouses, as well as hydraulic presses for compacting the heads of the tobacco hogsheads (barrels).

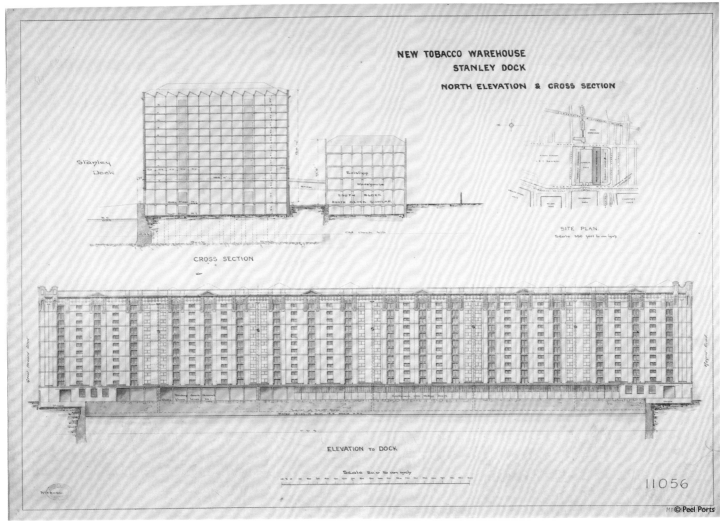

Drawing of elevation and section of Stanley Dock Tobacco Warehouse

The Tobacco Warehouse dominates the landscape and is visible from miles around. It extends the full length of the dock and is 14 storey high with 46 regular bays divided internally into six fire-proof compartments. Its construction used 27 million bricks, 30,000 panes of glass and 8,000 tons of steel. Three bridges link it to the south warehouse across what is known as 'Pneumonia Alley' because it is permanently in shade and its tendency to act as a wind tunnel.

As well as the principal warehouse buildings, there are a number of other important structures around the Stanley Dock. At the same time as the north and south warehouses were erected, Hartley built two hydraulic power stations, one on each side of the passage leading into the dock, only one of which now survives. This is a tall octagonal tower built of granite. It has narrow slit openings and castellations with a tall circular chimney. It was extended to the north and south when the south hydraulic power station was demolished to make way for the Tobacco Warehouse. It provided power for the lifting equipment, capstans and tobacco pressing machinery.

At the east head of the dock is the entrance to the Leeds and Liverpool Canal. Like the dock retaining walls, it is constructed of Cyclopean granite. Above it is a bridge with curved abutments.

HYDRAULIC POWER

Hydraulic power relies on pressurised water within a pipe. In early hydraulic systems, the pressure was created by reservoirs or by pumping water up into tanks at the top of very tall towers, such as the 200ft high tower at Grimsby Docks (1849). However, reservoirs needed a constant supply of water and the construction of such towers was very expensive. So in 1850 W G Armstrong developed the accumulator system, whereby a weight bin and water was pumped up a shorter tower by a steam engine and the fall of the weight bin by gravity was controlled to provide a constant supply of high pressure water. This effectively stored power against demand, ironing out cyclical variations in pressure from pumps or water supply. The pressurised water was transferred to the point of demand in iron pipes which fed into a jigger or hydraulic ram, consisting of a hollow cylinder, closed at one end and at the other is a sliding piston, forced to move when the water under pressure is admitted into the cylinder. The movement of the cylinder is transferred to a chain and the piston's travel is multiplied by the number of pulleys around which the chain passes.

It was Armstrong who designed the hydraulic machinery and accumulators used throughout Liverpool Docks. Jesse Hartley had heard about the success of Armstrong's hydraulically powered cranes in Newcastle, went to inspect them

Water was pumped to the top of this tower in order to create a constant pressure, which could be used in maintaining hydraulic power.

© John Hinchliffe

Tobacco Press in South Warehouse at Stanley Dock

and was so impressed by them and their operative John Thorburn (known to his friends as Hydraulic Jack) that he introduced himself to Armstrong and declared that '... the crane was just the thing for his docks' stating in a report to the Dock Board: '...I think it one of the most important acquisitions which can be given to warehouses and docks.' When Albert Dock was nearing completion, Hartley ordered two hydraulic lifts and two hydraulic cranes for the warehouses. Armstrong supplied two 5-ton lifts or hoists in 1848, at a cost of £500 each, followed a year later by two cranes for the quayside. These first installations drew their water from the Corporation mains water supply, via pipes originally of 7in diameter which were replaced by 12in pipes in 1850. All evidence of these early installation has disappeared.

In 1851 Armstrong submitted estimates for accumulators and their associated machinery to power cranes at Queens and Stanley Docks, Liverpool. For Queens, he offered to supply a 7 ton crane, a 12 horsepower high pressure engine, accumulating reservoir, cast iron pressure pipes, one 5,000 gallon capacity water cistern and other equipment for £1,660 plus a 15-ton crane. For Stanley Dock, the machinery was to include a '...hoisting machine with vibrating jib for raising coal boxes out of barges and delivering them into ships lying outside the same.' By March 1852, the estimate for Queens Dock had been accepted and the hydraulic crane was in operation. In April 1853 tenders were sought again for the hydraulic equipment for Stanley Dock. The tenders were accepted and the two accumulators were installed in the two new power stations to the north and south of Stanley Dock Gate in 1854.

Initially hydraulic power was used for specific pieces of equipment, such as cranes, but from the late 1850s the concept of central hydraulic power generating stations was introduced. The first at the Stanley Dock in 1854

was followed by Wapping Dock in 1856, then Birkenhead Docks in 1861, Herculaneum Dock in 1864, Albert Dock in 1878 and Bramley-Moore Dock in 1884. The technology was no longer pioneering when the building at Bramley-Moore Dock was erected, and by the 1930s, electric power had replaced hydraulic power throughout the docks, but the accumulator towers at Stanley Dock were amongst the very first to be built in the country, if not the world, and the surviving accumulator tower could be the oldest of its type in existence.

HERITAGE ACHIEVEMENTS SINCE INSCRIPTION

After a long period of dormancy since the closure of the central docks, a number of welcome initiatives have recently taken place. One is the return of water-based activities at the Collingwood Dock. Here the Glaciere Maritime Academy, in conjunction with the City of Liverpool College and site owners Peel Holdings, has established a rapidly-expanding programme of courses in sailing, diving and power-boating.

Peel has also initiated a programme of conservation for the most neglected buildings and structures within the area. To date, sections of the dock wall at Princes Dock and two of the police huts that back onto the dock wall at Collingwood Dock have been restored; there have been emergency works to various structures around the Clarence Graving Dock, many of the historic gateways and drinking fountains along the dock wall have been cleaned and repaired, and unsightly extensions to the Victoria Tower have been removed.

Bascule Bridge and North Warehouse at Stanley Dock

Bascule Bridge

Peel's biggest conservation project to date has been the restoration of the bridge which carries Regent Road over the passage between the Collingwood and Stanley Docks. This is a lifting bridge constructed by Dorman Long to replace an original swing bridge in 1932. It is constructed of steel girders with an elevated timber-clad engine house and rolling ballast-box, which acts as the balance for lifting the bridge. Originally it was operated by hydraulic power, but was later fitted with 26 hp electric motors. The Bascule Bridge (the word bascule comes from the French for see-saw) was closed to traffic in 2008 due to corrosion of the steel structure. After major structural repairs and refurbishment, it reopened in August 2010 and received an award from the Institute of Civil Engineers for the 'best bridge restoration'. While it no longer operates as a lifting bridge, the original hydraulic machinery and later electric turbines survive within the engine room in good condition, and it has been opened to the public during recent Heritage Open Days.

North Warehouse after restoration and conversion to hotel

Stanley Dock North Warehouse

The huge scale of the warehouses at Stanley Dock, their isolation from the city centre and their disuse for 30 years has presented a major challenge. Many proposals have been put forward over the years but only with the purchase of the ensemble by new owners in 2010 has any significant investment been put into the conservation and conversion of this remarkable group of buildings. The regeneration of the site began with the ambitious conversion of the North Warehouse into a 153 bedroom luxury hotel with spa and conference facilities. Work commenced on site in January 2013 by Abercorn Construction for Harcourt Developments and was completed in mid 2014. The work has been undertaken in accordance with conservation principles which aimed at preserving as much as possible of the historic fabric and character of the building. The expectation is that the remaining historic buildings within the site will also be conserved and converted and that they will act as a catalyst for the regeneration of the surrounding area of North Liverpool.

Existing Liverpool Waters site

IN NEED OF ATTENTION

Liverpool Waters

The land stretching from Princes Dock to Bramley-Moore Dock, bounded by the River Mersey and the dock boundary wall is known as Liverpool Waters. Covering an area of 60 hectares, it is the most important undeveloped area of redundant dockland remaining in Liverpool, of which over 40% is within the World Heritage Site. Outline planning permission was granted in 2013 by Liverpool City Council for a huge mixed-use development phased over 30 years, despite objections from English Heritage and UNESCO about the impact of certain elements of the proposal. The project offers unparalleled opportunities for economic and social regeneration, and potential heritage benefits include restoring the redundant docks and bringing them back to life with water-based activities and enhanced biodiversity. Ever since its reclamation from the river this expanse of waterfront has been closed to the public. The intention is that by opening it up with a river walk, new parks and open spaces, a historic quarter of the city centre will be revealed for the first time. While acknowledging these opportunities, English Heritage and UNESCO believe that it is essential that the scheme is carried out in a way that does not harm the Outstanding Universal Value of the World Heritage Site. These organisations have advised that buried archaeological remains of the once technologically-advanced central docks should be protected, and that special attention should be given to the mass and scale of development so that it does not unbalance the cityscape and detract from the prominence of the Pier Head buildings and the historic city centre.

'Pnuemonia Alley' between Tobacco Warehouse and Hartley's south warehouse

© P Graham

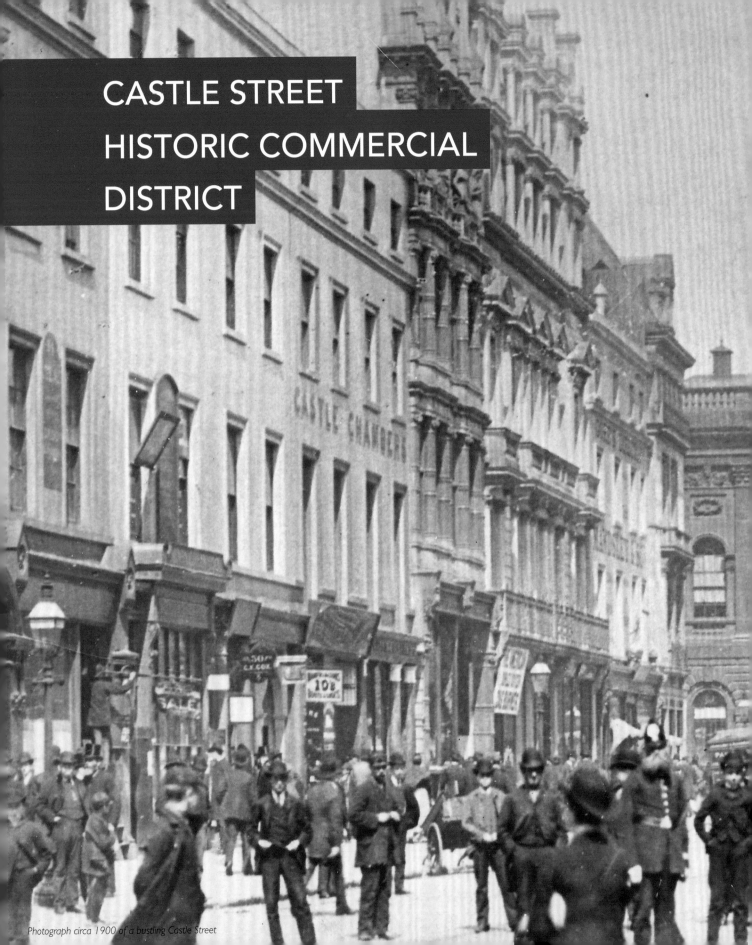

CASTLE STREET
HISTORIC COMMERCIAL
DISTRICT

Photograph circa 1900 of a bustling Castle Street

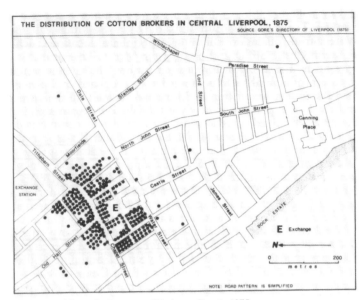

Distribution of Cotton Brokers around Exchange Flags in 1875

The historic commercial district has evolved continuously from the 18th century onwards, and is over-laid on Liverpool's seven medieval streets. It is home to historic banks, shipping-line headquarters, marine insurance companies, produce exchanges and warehouses, as well as the city's Georgian Town Hall and other civic and social buildings. Liverpool is a city built on trade and this is the area where business was conducted and where mercantile culture is most overtly displayed. The complete absence of medieval structures and the quality of their Georgian and Victorian replacements epitomise Liverpool's tradition of change, based on an irrepressible spirit of commerce and success in trade.

The area is still Liverpool's business centre, although changes in shipping and trading practices have resulted in many of the historic buildings becoming redundant. Some grand commercial buildings have been converted to new uses such as the Adelphi Bank on Castle Street, which now houses a coffee shop, and The Albany on Old Hall Street, with its prophetic inscription 'Time and tide tarry for no man' in the courtyard, which is now apartments.

A wide range of architectural styles and prestige material abound. With examples of early cast iron-framed buildings (Oriel Chambers, Water Street and 16 Cook Street), steel-framed buildings (Royal Insurance Building, North John Street) and American-influenced restrained classicism (India Buildings), this area demonstrates the important role of Liverpool in the evolution of building technology and design.

Sculpture of Mermaid and Merman holding a shield with a Liver Bird at high level on Martins Bank Building

Throughout the area are high quality sculptures, both free-standing, such as the Nelson Monument in Exchange Flags, and integral to buildings, as on Martin's Bank Building in Water Street, with its reliefs depicting Liverpool's early trade links with Africa. The only medieval evidence which can be seen at ground level is the Sanctuary Stone outside 14 Castle Street, which marked the boundary of the Liverpool Fair, within which debtors were immune from arrest.

The natural topography has influenced the character of the area. The land rises gently from the river to a low ridge along the line of Castle Street, dropping down again to the shallow depression along Whitechapel, which was the route of the Pool of Liverpool. The straightness of the streets and the sloping ground allow spectacular views through and out of the area, framed by the buildings, especially westwards to the river and eastwards to the cultural buildings of William Brown Street.

The historic townscape of the historic commercial district is created by a hierarchy of straight principal streets containing the most important commercial buildings and subsidiary thoroughfares, often at right angles, very narrow, lined by warehouses, and workshops. Vehicles are drawn down the principal streets but pedestrians can explore the surprising delights of the secondary routes such as Queen's Avenue and the Cavern Quarter, famous as a frequent venue for the Beatles and enlivened by statues of John Lennon and Eleanor Rigby.

Nelson Memorial

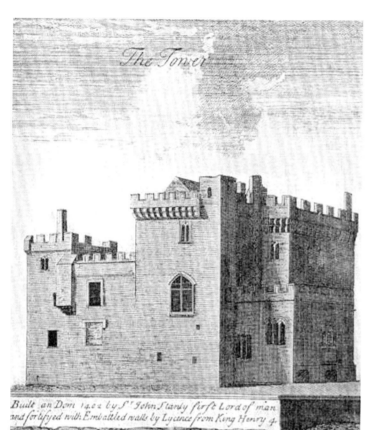

Tower of Liverpool

HISTORY

Shortly after Liverpool was founded in 1207, the town developed into a small settlement of seven streets forming an approximate H plan: They survive as Water Street, Castle Street, Chapel Street, Dale Street, High Street, Tithebarn Street and Old Hall Street. Although these medieval streets have all since been widened, they still form the basis of the historic commercial district.

The settlement grew little during the medieval period but it did acquire significant buildings: Liverpool Castle (1235), the Chapel of St Mary del Key (early 13th century), the Church of St Nicholas (1355) and the Tower of Liverpool (pre-1406). Settlers had been attracted by the offer of free burgage plots (narrow strips of land at the rear of the street frontage) in return for accepting civic responsibilities and paying taxes of one shilling per year. The width of these burgage plots is still reflected in places by narrow plot frontages to the principal streets.

After the Civil War, the town began to expand more rapidly, claiming by 1699 to be the third trading port in England, with ships sailing mainly to Ireland and along the British Coast but also to the Continent and America. With the continued increase in trade during the early 18th century, merchants were attracted and built new houses. Initially they remained close to the waterfront and conducted their business from home, often with an attached or nearby warehouse for goods. By the middle of the 18th century the Town Hall (1749-54) had been built as a focus for business, and several coffee houses had opened nearby where merchants could meet to conduct business and where public sales were held. The infilling of the Pool in 1710-15 enabled the city to expand southwards, and by the beginning of the 19th century merchants began to move away from the increasingly hectic streets of the old town.

The construction of the U shaped Exchange Buildings (1803-08, although rebuilt 1864-7 and 1939-55) and the formation of Exchange Flags at the rear of the Town Hall created large bespoke trading facilities and established the junction of Water Street, Dale Street, Old Hall Street and Castle Street as the focal point of the commercial district. The remarkable increase in trading activity in the 19th century led to all the medieval buildings and most 18th century buildings being replaced by banks, offices, showrooms and produce exchanges on the frontages of the principal streets and by warehouses on the secondary streets. By the 1870s the original medieval centre had virtually no dwellings and had become: '...a sphere to do business in, to make money or - to lose it...'

The narrow medieval streets were inadequate to accommodate the vast number of pedestrians and vehicles and, as the success of the port required goods to be transported to and from the docks, a series of road improvements began in 1786 with the widening of Castle Street. Victoria Street was cut through the town in the 1860s to provide another east-west route; its western end becoming the focus of the fruit and provisions trade.

Throughout the commercial district, the tradition was to employ the best architects and finest materials to create buildings that would impress both customers and competitors. These buildings were intended as symbols of power, recalling the glories of Renaissance Italy: '...a city of merchant princes bestowing their munificence upon vast palaces of commerce and fine civic buildings.'

During the second half of the 20th century and the beginning of the 21st century, the area continued to evolve as trading practices changed and some of the older commercial buildings became impractical for their original use. The focus of business activity shifted to new office accommodation centred on Old Hall Street. This has meant finding new uses for some of the older buildings such as apartments and hotels.

Drawing showing the widening of Castle Street in 1786

Aerial view of Castle Street before wartime destruction, showing domes of Town Hall and Foster's Customs House

HIGHLIGHTS

Castle Street

Before devastating war damage, Castle Street was twice its current length, and was terminated by the Custom House, the great domed building by John Foster Jnr. This provided a fitting counterpoint to the dome and portico of the Town Hall to the north, with the dome of the Queen Victoria Monument forming a centre-piece. The Custom House was demolished in 1948, but even in its truncated form, it remains one of the most impressive streets of predominantly Victorian commercial architecture in the country.

Liverpool Town Hall (1749-54; 1789-92; 1795-1820) is

the decision-making venue for Liverpool City Council, the official base of the Lord Mayor, the home of the Hall of Remembrance (for Liverpool's First World War dead) and a venue for major civic and social events. It is the city's finest Georgian building, and is the result of three building campaigns:
- the original design was by John Wood of Bath. At a time when Bath was seen as the one of most cultured towns in the country, Liverpool wanted to show that it too could display an interest in culture as well as commerce. The work was supervised by his son John Wood the Younger.
- additions and alterations were designed by James Wyatt and carried out by the elder John Foster in 1789-92;
- following a fire of 1795 it was reconstructed by Foster and Wyatt, the work continuing until c.1820.

Liverpool Town Hall in 2002, prior to repair and cleaning of stonework

It was built originally as an exchange, with an open arcade on the ground floor around a courtyard where business was conducted, and rooms for civic functions above. Wyatt added an extension to the rear, and his chaste Neo-classical north elevation overlooking Exchange Flags contrasts with the Palladian character of Wood's earlier work. Wyatt's dome was added in 1802, and the Corinthian south portico in 1811. Surmounting the dome is a Coade Stone figure identified variously as Minerva or Britannia, made by John Rossi in 1801-2. The richly carved friezes at high-level on the east and west elevations include exotic animals and races from around the world and celebrates the extent of Liverpool's foreign trade even in the mid-18th century, despite some bizarre sculptural depictions of animals which were unknown to the sculptors.

From the entrance hall, Wyatt's staircase rises under the dome. It leads to the magnificent first floor reception rooms. Overlooking Castle Street are three rooms with vaulted ceilings and refined decoration in the Wyatt manner. On the north side is the Large Ballroom with giant pilasters and an apsed niche for the band. The Dining Room has iron stoves and scagliola vases in imitation of porphyry. Most of the rooms have original chandeliers and furniture, and the whole ensemble is one of the best suites of civic rooms in the country. It is a powerful demonstration of the wealth of Liverpool at the opening of the 19th century.

The Town Hall effectively belongs to the people of Liverpool and so, although its continued use restricts access to organised tours, visitors are normally welcome to enter and admire the entrance hall, provided that functions are not impeded.

Town Hall Dome

Town Hall Dining room

Bank of England by Charles Cockerell

Bank of England (1845-48) is the largest and grandest of three Bank of England branch banks built in the mid-19th century and designed by C R Cockerell (the others are in Manchester and Bristol). It is a monumental composition in a blend of Greek and Roman Doric, every element majestically and boldly scaled. At the front are three bays, divided by fluted columns, the whole flanked by massive rusticated corner piers, and raised up on a rough granite plinth. The Castle Street frontage dramatically closes the views up Brunswick Street from the river. It is regarded as one of the masterpieces of Victorian commercial architecture - overwhelmingly massive, giving the impression of unshakeable confidence and security in the transactions of the banking business.

The Adelphi Bank (now Caffe Nero on the ground floor)

Parr's Bank (now Natwest)

Adelphi Bank (1890-92), now a coffee shop at ground floor level, is one of the more exotic buildings on Castle Street and was built to the design of W D Caroe. The façades combine bands of pink sandstone and pale grey granite, decorated in the manner of north European Renaissance architecture, mixed with Nordic and eastern European touches such as the treatment of the dormers and the green copper onion domes, to which the eye of the viewer is instantly attracted. The bronze entrance doors are by Thomas Stirling Lee, one of the principal sculptors to have worked on St George's Hall, with reliefs on the theme of brotherly love.

Parr's Bank (1900), now the Natwest Bank, is by Richard Norman Shaw (with Willink and Thinknesse) who had just completed the striking White Star Line offices in James Street. The building combines an unforgettable exterior with a plan of great functional clarity. The monumental classical façade relies on contrasts of colour, with bands of green and cream marble veneer interrupted by bright red terracotta window surrounds, all set above a two-storey granite plinth. The ground floor is occupied by a large circular banking hall, completely free from obstruction, lit by a shallow central dome. Above the dome, the upper offices are supported on massive iron girders to avoid crushing the delicate vault of the banking hall. It is an uncompromising statement about the prestige of the bank rather than polite street architecture.

Monument to Queen Victoria (1902-06) in Derby Square is built on the site of the old Liverpool castle and the subsequent 18th century St. George's Church. It was intended to represent the spirit of patriotism of Liverpool's citizens, as well as the national self-confidence that Victoria's long reign had engendered through the spectacular growth of the British Empire. The neo-Baroque Portland stone structure was designed by Professor F M Simpson of the Liverpool School of Architecture with Willink and Thicknesse. It provides an imposing setting for the colossal standing figure of the Queen, sculpted by Charles Allen, which is surrounded by allegorical groups representing Agriculture, Industry, Education and, most importantly for Liverpool, Commerce. The former presence of Liverpool Castle is recalled in a bronze relief plaque on the west side and, more subtly, the original location of the castle wall is picked out in darker paving in the north east corner of the square.

Nelson Memorial (1813) in Exchange Flags was Liverpool's first piece of free-standing outdoor sculpture and its chief instigator William Roscoe wanted a design of the highest artistic standard. The sculptor was Richard Westmacott, and the overall concept was by Matthew Cotes Wyatt. Funded by public subscription, the sculpture was intended to celebrate the growing prestige of Liverpool, and its location at the Exchange served to remind the city's merchants of the protection afforded to their commercial interests by Nelson's naval achievements. The somewhat macabre memorial shows Nelson receiving the Trafalgar battle honour from Victory, whilst Death reaches out to touch him with a skeletal hand. Four shackled prisoners in poses of anguish and dejection represent Nelson's four great victories at Cape St Vincent, the Nile, Copenhagen and Trafalgar. The memorial has been carefully conserved by National Museums Liverpool's sculpture conservation experts, using laser cleaning technology to remove the effects of pollution while retaining the patina of age.

Dale Street

Dale Street was first improved in 1786-90 after Castle Street had been widened. It was the principal route into and out of the town from London and Manchester. The north side was taken down in the 1820s and set back, and the construction of large commercial buildings began at the western end, around the Exchange, with the Queen Insurance Building of 1839 and the Liverpool and London Globe Insurance Building of 1855-57. As the century progressed, the buildings became increasingly large and imposing and spread further east.

Queen Insurance Building (1837-39) was commissioned from

the architect Samuel Rowland by the Royal Bank and was one of the earliest developments in Liverpool to include speculative offices for letting. It has a grand classical façade to Dale Street with a giant order of Corinthian columns and a tall balustraded cornice, surmounted by a large sculpture of the Royal Coat of Arms. A central passageway from Dale Street leads into Queen Avenue which is lined by shops and offices.

Royal Insurance Building (1897-1903) is on a strategic site

at the corner of Dale Street and North John Street. It is one of the finest of Liverpool's giant early 20th century office blocks. The architect, J. Francis Doyle, was selected by competition, the assessor being Norman Shaw, with whom Doyle had worked on the design of the White Star Building in James Street. Its Edwardian Baroque façade of Portland stone and granite conceals a revolutionary steel structure, one of the earliest uses of a steel frame in Britain. To provide a ground floor space unencumbered by columns, the upper floors are hung from great steel arches, braced to the structure above. The tower is embellished with a sundial and a gilded dome that glints over the city skyline, and the roof is crowded with dormers and massive chimneys. A series of sculpted panels by C J Allen at second floor level shows classically robed characters engaged in the world of insurance. It is a wonderfully assured design, a supreme example of a prestige national headquarters, unashamedly intended to impress. Empty for many years, it is being converted into a hotel.

Former Royal Bank, Queen Avenue

Royal Insurance Building undergoing restoration 2014

Sculpture of the Royal Coat of Arms on top of the parapet of Queen Building

Drawing of The Albany from Herdman's Modern Liverpool *(1864)*

135-139 Dale Street (1788) is a rare surviving terrace of late

Georgian houses, in the city centre, on a building line which predicted the early 19th century widening of Dale Street. The most impressive of the terrace is the corner property No. 139, which was built for John Houghton, a distiller, whose business works were adjacent on Trueman Street, and can still be recognised as a contemporary industrial building. The Trueman Street elevation of the house has a three-bay pediment and an Adam-style Venetian window at first floor. The terrace gives an indication of how Dale Street would have appeared at the end of the 18th century.

Old Hall Street

The Old Hall after which the street was named was the residence of the Moore family, and survived until the 1820s when the street was widened and warehouses and offices started to replace residences. When the first Exchange Buildings were erected in 1808, a labyrinth of courtyards and alleyways with densely built housing was cleared away. The construction of the Cotton Exchange in 1906 led to a slight shift of the centre of gravity of commercial activity away from the Exchange Buildings at the back of the Town Hall.

Albany Building (1856) was built as speculative offices by Richard

Naylor, a wealthy banker and Liverpool philanthropist, and designed by J K Colling. It combined three storeys of cellular offices with basement shops and warehousing. Adopting the form of an Italian palazzo with a central courtyard, it is given distinction by ornamentation based on Colling's passion for naturalistic plant forms and foliage carved in stone. The central gateway has excellent cast iron gates, made locally by Rankin's Union Foundry. Natural light is admitted to the building via top-lit glazed corridors. The building was used by cotton brokers for whom the courtyard served as a meeting place, and the quality of light in the offices provided good conditions for examining cotton samples. The side elevations are plainer but still have iron hoists for lifting goods into and out of the basement storage spaces. It is featured famously as the headquarters of Kit's employers in Thomas Armstrong's King Cotton. After years of disuse, it has been converted into apartments.

6, 8 and 10 Rumford Place (c.1840) is, architecturally, a

relatively undistinguished office building. Its primary significance is that it was the headquarters of James Dunwoody Bulloch and it became the unofficial Confederate Embassy in England during the American Civil War. Dunwoody was the Confederate Agent who commissioned cruisers to be built in England, mainly on Merseyside under the cover of the Southern Cotton Commissioners. The most famous of these ships was the CSS Alabama, built across the River Mersey at Lairds Shipyard in Birkenhead.

Water Street

Sloping dramatically down to the river, Water Street possesses some of Liverpool's most remarkable buildings of the 20th century. Charles Reilly said in 1921 that: 'Water Street is more like a ravine than a street.'

The third Tower Building on this site

Tower Buildings (1910) stands on the site of the Tower of Liverpool,

a fortified house belonging to the Stanley family, Earls of Derby, and used by them as an embarkation base for their property in the Isle of Man. The present Tower Buildings was designed by Aubrey Thomas, the Liverpool architect of the Royal Liver Building. It is similarly inventive, being one of the earliest steel-framed buildings in the country. The staircases are constructed on steel joists cantilevered out from the walls, thus removing the need for cranked strings, and the roofs, floors and partition walls are formed of reinforced hollow clay bricks. Above a robust plinth of granite, the material used to face the whole of the Liver Building, the building is clad in white Doulton terracotta in an attempt to cope with the polluted atmosphere of the city. Its facades, being largely undecorated, appear strikingly modern for its date, but it was not universally liked when built. Charles Reilly saw it as '...coarse classical detail...' and '...an incongruous admixture of equally bad Gothic.'

'Glass Bubbles' of Oriel Chambers

Oriel Chambers (1864) was designed by Peter Ellis, a Liverpool

architect. Oriel Chambers is a structure greatly ahead of its time and is now Liverpool's most celebrated office building, elevated to the status of a Modernist icon and described in the 1969 Pevsner as 'one of the most remarkable buildings of its date in Europe.' Liverpool had seen the use of cast iron framed buildings earlier in the 19th century in three churches, warehouses and in the much-mourned Liverpool Sailors' Home of 1852 but Oriel Chambers was possibly the first office building to employ this technique and the first to massively increase the window to wall ratio by introducing slender stone mullions and large oriel windows. The rationale for the oriel windows, framed in the thinnest sections of iron and with the maximum area of glass, was to provide good daylight for the office workers within. In the courtyard behind, the glazing forms a curtain wall, cantilevered out beyond the line of the frame. In its frank expression of function and technology, it influenced the young John Root, who was in Liverpool during its construction and he employed similar techniques when he began to practice in the commercial buildings of Chicago with Daniel Burnham. In its day, the building aroused much opposition. *The Porcupine*, a satirical magazine called it a 'vast abortion' and an 'agglomeration of protruding plate glass bubbles'. Ellis was also the architect of the nearby No. 16, Cook Street, built two years later. In its stripped aesthetic, it too is startlingly modern.

16 Cook Street

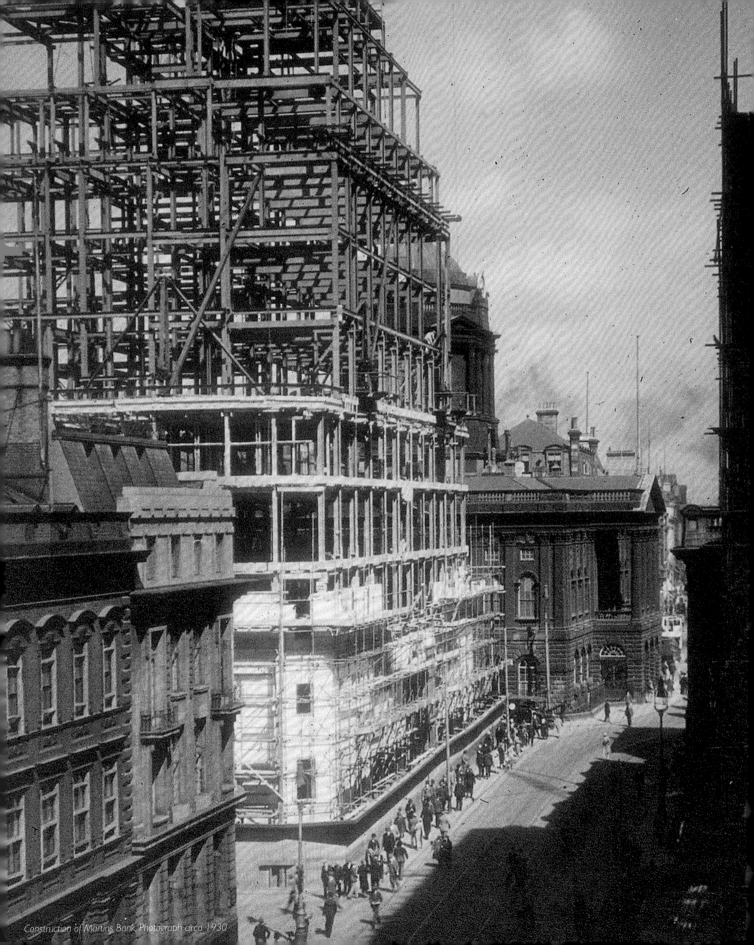

Construction of Martins Bank, Photograph circa 1930

India Buildings (1924-31)

India Buildings (1924-31) is the immense office building across the road from Oriel Chambers. It was built at a cost of £1,250,000 for Alfred Holt and Company's Blue Funnel Line, which traded predominantly with the Indian sub-continent, and bears witness to Liverpool's global trading connections. It was designed by Liverpool's greatest 20th century architect, Herbert J Rowse with Briggs, Wostenholme and Thorneley. Occupying a whole block between Water Street and Brunswick Street, it has stripped classical facades of great dignity and refinement, typical of North American architecture of the 1920s, with which Rowse was familiar following his study trips there. As such, it represents the continued evolution of office buildings which started in earnest with Oriel Chambers. Italian Renaissance detail is restricted to the top and bottom storeys. A barrel vaulted arcade flanked by shops runs through the centre of the ground floor, another American feature. The bronze lamps outside the entrance were made by the Bromsgrove Guild and were modeled on those of the Palazzo Strozzi, Florence. The building was badly damaged in the war, and restored under Rowse's supervision.

Martins Bank (1927-32)

Martins Bank (1927-32) on the opposite side of Water Street to India Buildings was also designed by Rowse and is acclaimed as one of the very best interwar classical buildings in the country. It is similarly monumental and American influenced and steps back at the upper levels to avoid dominating the lower surrounding buildings. The fine Art Deco-influenced sculpture by Herbert Tyson Smith with Edmund Thompson and George Capstick celebrates maritime themes, money and trade with Africa. The stylish top lit banking hall, with its Parisian jazz moderne fittings and extravagant use of colourful marbles, survives well, albeit currently unused, as does the boardroom on the eighth floor, which is decorated like the hall of a Renaissance palace, with a large chimneypiece and a painted, beamed ceiling. A further significance is that it is an early example of a completely ducted office building which incorporated a low temperature ceiling heating system.

Detail of painted ceiling in Boardroom of Martins Bank Building

Martins Bank Building

Victoria Street

In the 1860s Victoria Street was cut through an area of congested narrow streets to aid east-west communication. Large new buildings, mostly combining office accommodation and warehousing, were developed along it and the streets running off it. Generally these were built speculatively and provided storage for several different companies. Less celebrated than Castle Street or Dale Street, Victoria Street nonetheless preserves its 19th century character largely unaltered.

Fowler's Buildings

Fowler's Building (1865-69) was one of the first and finest of the substantial new building on Victoria Street. It was designed by Sir James Picton for Fowler Brothers, international dealers in foodstuffs. The frontage block of stone with polished granite columns housed the company offices, while behind it is a larger area of brick warehousing, part of which was reputedly used as a fish smokery. It is a nine-bay palazzo of local buff sandstone with a granite plinth and columns on the frontage, but the sides are much plainer, faced with polychromatic brick.

EXCHANGES AND SPECIALISED ZONES FOR COMMODITIES

Liverpool's commercial success was due in part to being a general cargo port. This role, rather than as a specialised port, meant that it was not wholly reliant on trade in any one commodity. The mainstays were the import of cotton, grain, tobacco, sugar and timber, and the export of coal, salt and manufactured goods, around the coast of Britain as well as internationally. The city's merchants and docks, however, were sufficiently flexible to support diversification of trade and the trans-shipment of almost any goods. Certain docks specialised in specific goods such as timber into Canada Dock, cotton into Albert Dock, corn into Waterloo Dock and coal out of Bramley Moore Dock. Similarly, specialised zones appeared within the historic commercial district where merchants in a particular commodity sought mutual benefit from being together.

The mercantile culture was based largely on open competition and free trade and this resulted in clustering of merchants' offices in well-defined areas of the historic business district. Potential customers could compare the quality and price of commodities from different suppliers with ease. Many of the principal commodities also had their own specific exchanges.

Cotton Exchange 1907

Cotton

The Town Hall, which initially incorporated an exchange, and subsequently the three bespoke incarnations of the Exchange at the back of the Town Hall, formed the principal hub of general trading activities, especially for the all-important trade of imported raw cotton during the 19th century. The plan on p.54 graphically illustrates the clustering of the cotton traders around the Exchange. Surviving examples of buildings which housed cotton traders are Mason's Building in Exchange Street East, the Albany Building in Old Hall Street and Berey's Building in Bixteth Street. When the new Cotton Exchange opened in Old Hall Street in 1906, the centre of gravity shifted slightly to the north.

The Cotton Exchange (1906) designed by Matear and Simon had a magnificent Edwardian frontage of Portland Stone columns and twin Baroque towers to Old Hall Street. Regrettably, the frontage was demolished in 1967, but the polished grey columns of Norwegian granite survive inside, as well as the original side and rear elevations. The elevation to Edmund Street is especially remarkable, consisting of huge classically detailed cast iron panels, made by the Macfarlane Foundry, Glasgow. The eroded sculpture on Old Hall Street represents the River Mersey, a further two in the courtyard represent Navigation and Commerce; all were salvaged from the original frontage. Orleans House in Bixteth Street, also by Matear and Simon employs a similar structural and cladding system and together these are evidence of Liverpool's continuing development of cast iron for building construction.

Although raw cotton is no longer imported into Liverpool in any significant volume, The International Cotton Association, the world's leading cotton trade association and arbitral body, is still based in Liverpool. It has recently moved its offices out of the Cotton Exchange back to its previous home in Exchange Buildings.

Corn Exchange

Corn

The first purpose-built Corn Exchange was built in Brunswick Street in 1808, rebuilt in 1853-4 and again in 1953-9. Although most of the corn merchants' offices have been demolished, the latest exchange and a pub bearing the name The Corn Market survive.

The Liverpool Corn Association was formed in 1853, six years after the abolition of the Corn Laws, to develop standards of trade conduct and fair dealing. It coincided with a sharp increase in imported grain, which had started in the second quarter of the century, due to the doubling of the population of Great Britain from 10 to 20 million between 1801 and 1851.

The surviving Corn Exchange (1953-9) was designed by the Liverpool-trained architect H Hinchliffe Davies and is an imaginative mix of stripped classism and mid-century form and massing. A full-plot podium accommodated the newsroom and trading floor, and set back stands a seven-storey block with cylindrical tank rooms on the roof. It is clad in Portland Stone and used some more unusual stones, such as aquagene tuff (also known as pillow lava breccias), regrettably currently painted over, and on the steps to Brunswick Street, a lower dark step of volcanic tuff from the Lake District and a top step of green-streaked marble, probably from Connemara.

Fruit and Produce

A concentration of merchants specialising in imported fruit and produce (including cured meats, tinned fish, butter and cheese) developed around the west end of Victoria Street, where the Produce Newsroom and Produce Exchange Buildings were subsequently built. The creation of Victoria Street coincided with the rapid expansion of the produce trade, which was partly driven by the rapid increase in the population of the North West, but also by the faster speed of steam ships and the spread of the railway network in both the USA and Europe, which enabled produce to be delivered to markets more quickly.

Produce Exchange Buildings (1902) by Henry Shelmerdine is

a big, vaguely Baroque edifice, curiously asymmetrical with a circular turret on the left and a gable surmounted by a pedimented niche on the right. The rear elevation onto Mathew Street is much less grand with plain brickwork and a large vehicular entrance to the goods depot for the Lancashire and Yorkshire Railway which occupied the ground floor.

The adjacent Fruit Exchange (circa 1888) was also built as a goods depot, for the London and North Western Railway, but was converted into an exchange by J B Hutchins in 1923. The frontage is in the Flemish Renaissance style, and inside on the upper floors, it retains its circular tiered sales rooms, where platforms rose up mechanically from the ground floor laden with samples of the produce being sold.

Gate on Commercial Saleroom Building

Commercial Saleroom Buildings (1879) was designed by J F

Doyle for wholesale auctions of imported fruit, and the great volume of this activity led to the creation of the Fruit Exchange across Temple Court. It is in the Queen Anne style in pressed red brick and is crowned by a frieze carved with swags and a balustraded parapet. The quality of the decorative wrought ironwork is especially high with delicate balconies and gates.

Lawyers and Accountants

Lawyers and accountants, essential for regulating transactions, were concentrated around Cook Street, Harrington Street and North and South John Street.

Heywoods Bank with manager's accommodation at rear

Financial Services

Banks were needed as places to deposit the huge proceeds of trade and to finance ventures. Castle Street and the streets leading from it was the centre for banks and other financial services. One of the first purpose-built banks in the country was the private bank of Messrs Heywood on the corner of Brunswick Street and Fenwick Street, c. 1800. It also had living accommodation for the bank manager at the rear.

Insurance

While great profits were made from trading, it was a risky business, with the potential for financial disaster, not least due ships lost at sea and fluctuating prices. Insurance for trading ventures was therefore an important part of the mercantile culture and Liverpool housed the headquarters of many marine (and other) insurance companies. They clustered in Castle Street and at the west end of Dale Street. The Royal Insurance Company built its first head office in 1848, and in the 1850s came the Liverpool and London Insurance Company and the Queen Insurance Company. Others followed including the British and Foreign Marine Company, the Prudential, Eagle Star and of course the Royal Liver Friendly Society.

Shipping Companies

Shipping companies commissioned the construction of ships, established trading routes and organised the trans-shipment of both goods and people. Understandably, they gravitated towards the river, so that they could easily get to the docks to inspect the goods and sell tickets to prospective emigrants. Major concentrations of shipping offices formed in Water Street and James Street. Most occupied speculative office buildings such as Tower Buildings and India Buildings, but some, such as Cunard and the White Star Line commissioned their own showpiece buildings and used them as advertisements for their business.

The White Star Line Building (1895-8) was designed by Richard Norman Shaw, with the local architect James F. Doyle overseeing construction. This eight storey steel-framed structure dominates the corner of The Strand and James Street, and ushered in the craze for tall office buildings in Liverpool. Stylistically, it is similar to Shaw's earlier New Scotland Yard in London with its use of alternating bands of red brick and white Portland Stone, and has domed turrets on The Strand elevation. Its tall gable was rebuilt in simplified form following war damage. The entire ground floor served as a booking hall with exposed, boldly riveted cast iron stanchions like the engine room of a ship, and a fire-proof ceiling of terracotta panels by J C Edwards of Ruabon. The building was disused for many years but has recently been restored and opened as a Titanic-themed hotel.

The White Star Line Building, now a hotel

The White Star Line Building interior 1898

WHAT THEY SAID

William Combe, *The Tour of Dr Syntax in Search of the Picturesque* 1809:

'…Liverpool, that splendid mart,
Imperial London's counterpart,
Where wand'ring Mersey's rapid streams
Rival the honours of the Thames,
And bear, on each returning tide,
Whate'er by commerce is supplied,
Whate'er the winds can hurry o'er
From ev'ry clime and distant shore.'

Anon, mid-19th century:

'They bought themselves new traps and drags,
They smoked the best cigars,
And as they walked the Exchange Flags,
They thanked their lucky stars.'

Carl Jung, *Memories, Dreams, Reflections* 1927

'I found myself in a dirty, sooty city. It was night, and winter, and dark and raining. I was in Liverpool.'

'Everything was extremely unpleasant, black and opaque- just as I felt then. But I had had a vision of unearthly beauty, and that was why I was able to live at all. Liverpool is the 'pool of life.' The 'liver', according to an old view, is the seat of life- which makes to live.'

HERITAGE ACHIEVEMENTS SINCE INSCRIPTION

The historic commercial district has benefited from massive public investment in the pavements, streets and squares, and private investment in the restoration and upgrading of many of the historic buildings.

Castle Street

A comprehensive street improvement scheme was undertaken to enhance the historic character by widening the pavements, reducing the width of the carriageway and cutting vehicular traffic. The pavements were resurfaced with York stone, with seats but not trees so that the street retains its historic urban character.

Pioneer Building

The city block west of Vernon Street still comprises four narrow buildings which reflect the historic burgage plots of ancient Liverpool. In 2010 the block was occupied by buildings of varying age and design: the Vernon Pub (circa 1840), a three-storey stuccoed building; Pioneer Building (circa 1910), a five-storey Arts and Crafts building in red brick with stone dressings; an undistinguished building of the 1950s; and Eagle Star House (circa 1935). Only the Vernon was occupied and even that was in need of repair. The vacancy of the other three buildings created an air of decay in the whole vicinity. The City Council worked with the owners and their advisors to agree a highly successful hotel development which retained the effect of the four plots, refurbished the best elements of the block, and introduced an exciting yet sympathetic new building in place of the 1950s building. The new scheme has brought activity back to this part of Dale Street.

IN NEED OF ATTENTION

Dale Street Shops

At the east end of Dale Street, opposite Municipal Building stands a short terrace of five three-storey buildings dating from circa 1820. The buildings represent the last surviving example of modest Georgian buildings in Dale Street, before developments began to assume much larger scale. Until recently, it was thought they were built as houses and subsequently converted to shops, but research by English Heritage indicates that they were purpose built as shops and are probably the oldest remaining in Liverpool.

Regrettably the buildings are in an advanced state of decay, unused and severely at risk. They are owned by Liverpool City Council, which is looking to find a suitable development partner to take over the buildings, and bring them back into beneficial use. The Main Bridewell at the rear of the shops is being converted to student accommodation after several years of disuse and so attention is now needed on the shops themselves.

© John Hinchliffe

Pioneer Building forms part of Ibis Hotel development on Dale Street

WILLIAM BROWN STREET
CULTURAL QUARTER

Painting of St George's Hall shortly after its opening in 1854 with the forum on St George's Plateau

This area was not part of the working port city but is included within the World Heritage Site as a testament to Liverpool's exceptional maritime mercantile culture. It was transformed in the mid-19th century by a radical municipal initiative to clear away the haphazard structures along the frontages and create a new cultural forum at the point of arrival by road and rail. Occupying the high ground above the old city centre, the centrepiece is St. George's Hall (1840-55), universally acclaimed as one of the greatest Neo-classical buildings in Europe. Along the northern edge is the imposing sequence of public buildings comprising the former County Sessions Court, the Walker Art Gallery, the Picton Library, the Museum and the former College of Technology, all built in the second half of the 19th century.

The display of fine architecture, statuary and cultural activities demonstrate the great wealth created by the mercantile trade, and the desire on the part of successful merchants and businessmen to spend that wealth in philanthropic gestures. This private benevolence in turn was matched by the determination of the Corporation to foster civic values and provide the most impressive venues for cultural activities. The great cultural collections and statuary (both in the museum, library and art gallery, and outside in the streets and squares) are of the highest calibre.

The area is bounded to the east and west by two transport structures which are internationally significant. In 1836 Lime Street Station became the terminus of the Liverpool and Manchester Railway, the world's first passenger line, and its North Shed had the widest span (200ft) of any building in the world when it was built in 1867. The portal of the Queensway Tunnel, which dates from 1934, is the principal entrance to what was the world's longest (2.14 miles) underwater road tunnel.

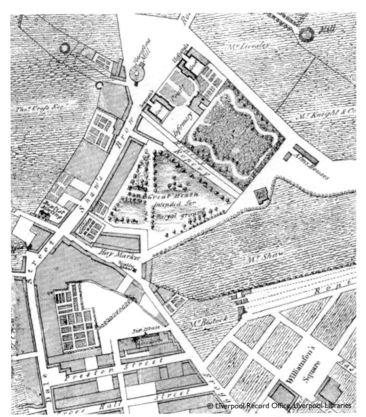

Plan of William Brown Street in late 18th century when it was Shaws Brow

HISTORY

Until the beginning of the 18th century, this was an area of heathland, beyond the limits of the town. Shaw's Brow, effectively the current William Brown Street, was the continuation of Dale Street and was one of the principal coaching roads into and out of the town. During the 18th and early 19th centuries, both sides of Shaws Brow had developed with a miscellany of windmills, lime kilns (hence the name of Lime Street), cottages, court dwellings, inns and potteries. As the population grew, the Liverpool Infirmary (1749) was built to the south east of Shaw's Brow, and St. John's Church (1784) was built behind the frontage properties to the south west. With the opening of Lime Street Station in 1836, the Corporation began the comprehensive redevelopment of the area to create the planned environment that we see today. It held a competition in 1839 for a concert hall and ultimately this led to the completion of St George's Hall on the site of the infirmary, followed in turn by the other cultural buildings.

Steble Fountain with Walker Art Gallery beyond

St John's Church was demolished at the end of the 19th century, and replaced by St John's Gardens which was laid out to provide a setting for memorials to Liverpool's leading citizens and social reformers. But in the 20th century, the civic grandeur was allowed to be spoilt by traffic encircling Lime Street, William Brown Street and St Johns Lane, denying its status as 'the finest civic parade in Britain'. In the 1970s William Brown Street was closed to traffic, and suitably resurfaced in granite and sandstone. While more could be achieved to enhance the area further, the magnificence of the buildings can again be appreciated.

St Georges Hall

HIGHLIGHTS

St George's Hall (1840-55) is an architectural masterpiece, described by Norman Shaw as "a building for all times, one of the great edifices of the world." Its creation was the result of a long-standing desire for a concert hall, for which a competition was held and won by the little-known, young prodigy architect from London, Harvey Lonsdale Elmes. At the same time, the Corporation held another competition for new Assize Courts on adjacent land closer to Lime Street Station. Elmes won again and soon the two projects were combined into one building.

Elmes died in 1847, probably exhausted by his efforts, before the hall was completed, leaving it in the hands of the architect, and family friend Charles Robert Cockerell. Cockerell made changes to Elmes' proposals for the internal decoration, notably by introducing more elaborate decoration, as can be appreciated by comparing his treatment of the Great Hall with Elmes' more restrained North Entrance Hall. Work began in earnest in 1841 and, despite Elmes' death, was carried through to completion in 1855 when its opening was celebrated with three days of concerts.

St George's Hall's free neo-Grecian exterior encloses a richly adorned Roman interior: a great rectangular tunnel-vaulted hall, inspired by the Baths of Caracalla in Rome, bounded by the two courts to north and south, which are linked by corridors running along the hall's long sides. At the south end of the building, where the ground falls away Elmes placed a great portico, with a double row of eight Corinthian columns, The formal entrance stands at the top of flights of steps designed by Cockerell and a tall retaining wall to St Johns Lane, which now houses the entrance to the visitor centre. The building proclaims Liverpool's aspiration for a civic forum with the Latin inscription on the frieze of the portico: Artibus Legibus Consiliis Locum Municipes Constituerunt Anno Domini MLCCCXLI (For Arts, Law and Counsel the townspeople built this place in 1841). The pedimented south entrance is a foil for the east elevation, where an even greater, thirteen-bay portico topped by an attic, allows entry into the long, eastern tunnel-vaulted corridor that gives access to the Great Hall and the courts.

The north front has an apse, through which a much smaller entrance leads to the North Hall and the Small Concert Room above it. The west side of the building lay very close to the now-demolished St John's Church and so is flatter and less decorated than the other elevations.

The Great Hall in St George's Hall with the Minton Tiles exposed

The Great Hall's sumptuously decorated interior celebrates the Corporation of Liverpool and its port, as well as its dedicatory saint. The panels of the vault include the Coat of Arms of Liverpool, Greek and Roman symbols of commerce and authority (the caduceus and fasces), mermaids and tridents. The vault is supported on massive red granite columns with spandrels containing figures portraying the qualities Victorian Liverpool aspired to: Fortitude, Prudence, Science, Art, Justice and Temperance. The Minton Hollins encaustic tile floor repeats the coat of arms and incorporates the mythical Liver Bird, Neptune, sea nymphs, dolphins and tridents. The tiled floor is covered most of the time to protect the tiles and to enable more flexible use of the Great Hall, although a small viewing panel has been formed and the whole floor is usually unveiled for viewing once a year.

The huge bronze doors, the pendant lights and stained glass continue the decorative theme of the grandeur of the port of Liverpool. Famously, the monogram SPQL, 'the Senate and People of Liverpool' is incorporated into the doors, as a reference to the ancient Roman monogram SPQR, highlighting Liverpool's imperial aspirations. Statues of Liverpool's great men are seen on either side of the Hall, including William Ewart Gladstone, Liberal statesman and four times Prime Minister, Samuel Robert Graves, merchant and ship owner and Joseph Mayer, principal benefactor of the Liverpool Museum. The City Council has recently commissioned and displayed a statue of Kitty Wilkinson, a lowly immigrant from Londonderry who went on to open Britain's first public washhouse on Upper Frederick Street in 1842. Although not part of Elmes' plan,

St Georges Hall small concert room

the massive organ, built by Henry Willis in 1855, and raised up on a semi-circular balcony, is one of the finest examples of this popular Victorian musical instrument in Britain.

The decoration of the semi-circular Small Concert Room is equally rich but more refined. It is entirely the work of Cockerell and was described by Charles Reilly as '...one of the loveliest interiors in the world'. Its colour palette is restrained: white, cream, honey, with touches of gilt and blue; its plasterwork includes the beautiful caryatids supporting the gallery. The cast iron lattice panels are exceptional for the undulating effect created by their outward swell.

The building was served by a sophisticated heating and ventilation system designed by Dr Boswell Reid. This circulated warm or cool air through insulated ducts, propelled by giant fans and controlled by man-operated canvas flaps. The organ too was originally linked to the heating and ventilation system, its bellows powered by the same steam engine that drove the fans.

Formal occupation by the courts, which had gradually dominated the use of the Hall in the 20th century, ceased in 1984 when new facilities opened elsewhere in the city. In 1993 the Hall reopened for public use and following a major scheme of repair and adaptation to maximise public access and use, at a cost of £23m, it was officially reopened on St George's Day, 23 April 2007.

© Peter de Figueiredo

William Brown Museum and Library

William Brown Museum and Library (1857-60) was the

next project in the creation of an ambitious cultural centre. A competition was held in 1855 for a new museum and public library, which was won by Thomas Allom. His scheme was too costly, so was later modified by the Corporation Surveyor John Weightman. Even so, the project went over budget and the financial difficulties were only overcome by the generosity of William Brown, the local MP, who had made a fortune in Liverpool as a merchant and banker, and agreed to meet the cost. The building opened to great acclaim in 1860 when 400,000 people attended the ceremony. Brown received a knighthood and Shaw's Brow was renamed in his honour.

It is a restrained and well-proportioned classical composition in the manner of St Georges Hall, with a deep central portico. Originally an elevated plateau with steps on either side gave access to the front of the portico but in 1902 this was replaced with the present wide and dramatic flight of steps, which now complete the ensemble. The Museum was extended to the south at the end of the 19th century into the upper floors of the new College of Technology (see below).

Bombing in 1941 resulted in the loss of most of the interior of the 1860 building but the principal elevation to William Brown Street elevation survived. The interior of the library was rebuilt 1957-60 and was extended to the rear in 1978. The interior of the museum was rebuilt in 1963-69 but by the beginning of the 21st century both the library and the museum proved to be inadequate. The museum was redesigned by National Museums Liverpool and re-opened in 2005 with an impressive six-storey atrium in a former service well and enlarged display galleries, incorporating the whole of the former College of Technology which fronts onto Byrom Street. It was renamed World Museum Liverpool to reflect the international strength of its collections which were the result of the city's global trading connections.

The library has also been remodelled and re-opened in 2013 with a spectacular new atrium designed by Austins-Smith:Lord Architects.

Liverpool Central Library atrium

The Picton Reading Room

Liverpool Central Library, which now incorporates the rebuilt William Brown Library, the Picton Reading Room and the Hornby Library, has undergone a massive transformation by architects Austin Smith: Lord for Liverpool City Council. It re-opened in 2013, with a further rebuild of the William Brown Library behind the front elevation, modern library facilities, a dramatic full-height atrium befitting the exterior of the building and a roof-top viewing terrace.

Walker Art Gallery (1877) also bears witness to the philanthropic tradition of successful businessmen giving benefactions to make art accessible to the public. It is named after its principal benefactor, Andrew Barclay Walker, Lord Mayor of Liverpool, who had made his fortune in brewing. It was originally used for the display of contemporary art but it rapidly acquired a permanent collection of historic paintings and sculpture worthy of a national gallery. The tradition of supporting contemporary art was revived in 1957 with the foundation of the prestigious biennial John Moores Painting Prize which continues to showcase the best work being done today throughout the country.

The building was designed by architects Sherlock and Vale. The classical portico is surmounted by a personification of Liverpool, holding a trident, sitting on a bale of cotton, supporting a ship's propeller and with a Liver Bird in attendance. To each side of the entrance are greater than life-size figures of Raphael and Michelangelo by John Warrington Wood. The building was extended in 1884, again at the expense of Sir Andrew Barclay Walker, who was knighted for his generosity, and again in 1931-33 by Sir Arnold Thornley. The interiors underwent a major refurbishment in 2001-2.

Picton Reading Room (1875-79) is an early addition to the library, designed by Cornelius Sherlock. It was funded by Liverpool Corporation and named after Sir James Picton, a prolific Liverpool architect and sometimes outspoken antiquarian, who was Chairman of the Library and Museums Committee. Its circular plan was influenced by the British Museum Reading Room (1854-57). The semi-circular façade ingeniously disguises the change in direction and ground level of William Brown Street at this point. The drum-like exterior, surrounded by detached Corinthian columns, was intended to echo Greek and Roman temples. However in the minds of Victorian Liverpudlians it suggested a more prosaic structure and became known as Picton's Gasometer. The circular reading room retains its original bookcases, cast iron gallery and large central lamp, which was lit by electricity from the beginning.

Hornby Library (1906) is an extension to the library, funded by Hugh Frederick Hornby, a merchant who specialised in trade with Russia, to house his collection of rare books and prints. The impressive stone-faced Edwardian Baroque interior was designed by the Corporation Surveyor Thomas Shelmerdine.

The Walker Art Gallery surmounted by 'The Spirit of Liverpool'

Former County Sessions Court, now part of National Museums Liverpool

County Sessions House (1882-1884) occupies the plot at
the top of William Brown Street and closes the vista at the north east end of St George's Plateau. It was built to house the Quarter Sessions, which heard cases involving non-capital offences and were tried by magistrates. As such it complemented the law courts in St George's Hall. The architects, F & G Holme, provided a building housing three courtrooms, complex circulation routes and attendant facilities, from barristers' library to cells, which has remained virtually unchanged since it opened. The external design continues the classical theme established by the earlier buildings on William Brown Street, but is inspired more by Renaissance Venice than ancient Greece and Rome. The Courts Act of 1971 abolished Quarter Sessions and the building is now in the care of National Museums Liverpool.

Former College of Technology on lower two floors, now all part of the World Museum Liverpool

Former College of Technology and Museum Extension
(1896-1901) occupies the plot at the bottom of William Brown Street.
Its original main entrance was on Byrom Street, with delightful Art Nouveau figures by F W Pomeroy forming the lamps at the base of the steps. By the end of the 19th century the museum collections had grown, and the Corporation decided to combine the urgent need for more storage and display space with

the demand for a new School of Science, Technology and Art. A competition was held in 1896 and won by the London architect, William Mountford. His design is more Edwardian Baroque than purely Classical, but it integrates harmoniously with its earlier neighbours. The dual use of college and museum was accommodated at two levels, skilfully reflected in the exterior decoration.

During major refurbishment and extension of the Museum in 2001-05, the main entrance to the World Museum Liverpool was created in the centre of the William Brown Street frontage. The Observatory Tower incorporated into the building, complete with domed roof with sliding panels, and The Planetarium within it had a major re-vamp in 2012 to include a new digital projection system, which has transformed the planetarium's shows.

Lime Street Station (1867-79) became the west terminus of the
Liverpool and Manchester Railway when it opened in 1836, six years after the opening of the line. The railway was crucial to the success of the port, facilitating the regular and rapid movement of goods to and from the city and also bringing in millions of emigrants from across the country and Europe en route to the waterfront. The station was sited at the end of the long cutting and tunnel through the red sandstone ridge which separated it from Edge Hill Station. The present station comprises two parallel sheds each covered by a wide curved iron and glass roof. The north shed was begun in 1867 and, at the time, was the widest in the world with a span of 200 feet. The engineers were W Baker and F Stevenson. The almost identical south shed was completed in 1879.

Former North West Hotel/Lime Street Chambers. Note the former Concourse House (demolished 2009) to the right

Lime Street Chambers (former North Western Hotel)
(Opened 1871) was designed by Alfred Waterhouse to serve passengers
using Lime Street Station. Its French Renaissance style with a romantic roofline is at odds with the Classical theme used elsewhere in the area but its scale and symmetry create a strong backdrop to the fine assembly of civic buildings. Waterhouse's original design was for a brick building, but the Corporation donated funds for it to be faced in stone.

Drawing of lamp erected at entrance to the Queensway Tunnel (now demolished)

Main Entrance to the Mersey Tunnel (1925 – 1934),

the first road tunnel under the river following the railway tunnel of 1886. Sir Basil Mott and J A Brodie engineered the road tunnel but the entrances and associated ventilation shafts, prodigious structures in themselves, were designed by the architect Herbert J Rowse. Although the style may differ from the cultural buildings, the architectural quality of the tunnel portal and associated elements are by no means out-shone by their grander neighbours. Rowse's distinctive stripped Classical style is best seen in the two pylons to left and right of the sweeping entrance walls. These resemble triumphal arches with fluted columns whose bases, capitals and entablatures draw on stylised representations of the River Mersey. Wavy lines also occur as part of the cornice of the entrance walls and above the tunnel opening. A shield over the portal itself includes a winged wheel and a pair of winged bulls, symbolising swift and heavy traffic. All are in white Portland Stone.

The bronze statues, by Sir W Goscombe John, of King George's V and Queen Mary, who opened the tunnel were repositioned one on either side of the retaining walls, as their original location, facing Dale Street, had been obscured by a controversial modern fly-over. A major loss was the demolition of a great black granite lighting column which marked the approach to the entrance, although it is rumoured to have survived, buried in a landfill site. The corresponding column in Birkenhead remains, albeit dislocated from the immediate tunnel entrance.

Segantini's The Punishment of Lust

COLLECTIONS AND SCULPTURE

The wealth created by the port, docks, shipping and related trade enabled public and private accumulation of collections and their public display throughout the cultural forum. The erection and first extension of the Walker was funded by the Walker brewing family. The gallery gained additional bequests from George Audley, son of a ship-builder who specialised in the export of beer and whiskey, to extend the gallery in 1930. He donated over 80 important Victorian paintings. In 1923 James Smith, an importer of Mediterranean wines bequeathed six sculptures by Rodin, 28 paintings by G F Watts and other works. The Holt family, owners of the Blue Funnel Line, gave several important paintings and the P H Holt Trust continues to support the Walker. The Walker's outstanding Old Master paintings include early Italian and Flemish works from the collection of the banker and abolitionist William Roscoe, who dreamed of making Liverpool a European cultural centre to rival Renaissance Florence. The Naylor family of bankers gave many portraits and a major French 19th century picture by Ary Scheffer. Philip Henry Rathbone, a member of one of Liverpool's most important nonconformist and radical merchant dynasties, was an influential chairman of the Arts and Exhibitions Committee, and led the purchase of the avant-garde Italian masterpiece The Punishment of Lust by Segantini. A more recent major donor of works of art was the retail and football pools magnate Sir John Moores

The Sculpture Gallery in The Walker

William Brown, a linen trader, general merchant and banker, funded the construction of the Liverpool Museum (now World Museum Liverpool), initially with the primary purpose of housing the 13th Earl of Derby's outstanding natural history collection. The initial collections in the museum have since been augmented by antiquities, ethnographic artefacts, and botanical, geological and entomological reference materials from around the world, many brought back by the city's sailors and merchants. The most notable mercantile benefactor was Arnold Ridyard, Chief Engineer of the Elder Dempster line. Between 1895 and 1916 he bequeathed 2,500 ethnological objects collected on his voyages from Liverpool to West and Central Africa. Over time, the collections came to reflect the ports of call of the Elder Dempster ships, mapping some of the key European trading routes on the coastline.

- **The Wellington Memorial (1861-30)**, a 40 metre high fluted Doric column surmounted by a bronze statue of the Iron Duke by G A Lawson
- **The Steble Fountain (1877-79)** by Paul Lienard, a circular stone basin with a cast iron centrepiece with marine figures reclining beneath two smaller basins from which water tumbles out of a mermaid's shell and fish masks.

Detail of a page from Audubon's Birds of America

Detail of Cenotaph

Liverpool Central Library has amassed a hugely impressive collection of medieval manuscripts and rare books. These include the 'double elephant folio' of Audubon's Birds of America, which is on permanent display, with pages turned regularly so that all the exquisite, life-size hand-coloured prints can be appreciated. The Hornby Library, built to accommodate the donation of rare books and prints from the Hornby family of Liverpool merchants, makes a fine showcase for these collections.

The William Brown Street Cultural Quarter enjoys a massive concentration of sculpture of the highest quality. This includes those within the buildings, notably the Sculpture Gallery in the Walker Art Gallery and in St George's Hall, and outside, such as the panels along the east elevation of St George's Hall which tell the stories of national prosperity and Liverpool's growth. In addition there are many free-standing monuments, the most notable of which are listed below.

Monuments in St George's Plateau

- Bronze equestrian statue of Prince Albert (1866) by Thomas Thornycroft
- Bronze equestrian statue of Queen Victoria (1870) by Thomas Thornycroft
- Benjamin Disraeli, the Earl of Beaconsfield and Prime Minister,(1883), who said that Liverpool was 'the second city of the British Empire', by C B Birch
- Major-General Earle (1887) native of Liverpool and leader of British Imperial campaigns in India and Africa by Birch
- The Cenotaph (1930) by Lionel Budden, to the fallen of the First World War, a large rectangular block of stone with bronze relief panels of marching soldiers and mourning civilians by Tyson Smith

Tyson Smith's sculptural panel of the families left at home on Budden's Cenotaph

Monument to William Ewart Gladstone, four times Prime Minister

Ai Weiwei's spider's web of light over Exchange Flags

St John's Gardens and Its Monuments

- Alexander Balfour (1889), champion of destitute sailors and their families, by A Bruce Joy
- William Rathbone (1899), founder of the District Nursing movement and the universities of Liverpool and Wales, by George Frampton;
- Sir Arthur Bower Forwood (1903), merchant, shipowner, Mayor and MP, by Frampton
- William Ewart Gladstone (1904), four times Prime Minister and native of Liverpool, by Sir Thomas Brock
- Monsignor James Nugent (1906), founder of boys schools and supporter of Irish and other poor emigrants who passed through Liverpool, by F W Pomeroy
- Canon T Major Lester (1907), founder of ragged schools and children's homes in Liverpool by Frampton
- Monument to the King's Liverpool Regiment (1905) by Sir W Goscombe John

Artists and craftspeople have made an important contribution to the fabric and cultural life of the city. Building on the success of Liverpool's year as European Capital of Culture in 2008, this tradition is continued by involving contemporary artists of national and international reputation in the design of public spaces and new regeneration schemes. Artists play an important role by engaging with local communities, bringing fresh insights to the city's heritage and promoting a positive image of Liverpool as a place that embraces change. Jorge Pardo's playful cluster of lighting columns, Penelope, inspired by Homer's Odyssey, for example, gives new meaning to Wolstenholme Square. Temporary events and installations supported by Liverpool's cultural programme, such as Ai Weiwei's spider spinning a web of light across Exchange Flags, also help to make the city's spaces more enjoyable and memorable.

These publicly commissioned sculptures are significant as individual works of art but collectively, they are a reflection of the city's self-image and identity. They are a graphic reminder of the roots of Liverpool's mercantile maritime role.

WHAT THEY SAID

Charles Dickens gave many readings in St George's Hall and described it as:

'...the most perfect hall in the world'.

Dickens often performed in the small concert room and he commented that before an appearance in 1866:

'...enthusiasm had reached the highest pitch' and the hall was besieged by a huge crowd, so that '...it looked at one time as if those who had tickets could not get in, and those who had not tickets could not get out'.

George Dolby, organised Charles Dickens's later reading tours:

'…the good feeling of the people of Liverpool showed itself heartily in the street; for during his (Charles Dickens's) progress to the station, he was repeatedly stopped by persons of the working classes wanting to shake hands with him, and all of them eager to thank him for the pleasure his books had afforded them.'

HERITAGE ACHIEVEMENTS SINCE INSCRIPTION

Most of the historic buildings within the William Brown Street Cultural Quarter have received significant investment since inscription from the responsible public authorities to ensure their proper repair and maintenance. The state of conservation of this area is therefore exceptionally high. The careful stewardship of these major historic assets, notably by Liverpool City Council, National Museums Liverpool and Network Rail is a clear indication that they accept their responsibility as custodians of the World Heritage Site.

Lime Street Station Gateway

One major achievement has been the enhancement of the approach to Lime Street Station, which is not only the principal railway station in the city but a significant historic building in its own right. At the time of inscription, the frontage of the South Shed was almost entirely obscured by Concourse House, a 13 storey tower built in 1967-68 on the corner of Lime Street and Skelhorne Street and a curved row of single storey shops. This restricted access to side entrances or a narrow set of steps from Lime Street. A scheme was developed that removed the shops and tower, replacing them with a sweeping elliptical arrangement of steps and ramp, reflecting the simple classical approach adopted in William Brown Street and St George's Plateau. The layout helps to direct pedestrians to their destinations, either directly to the main retail area, or to the commercial quarter and waterfront. Steps at higher levels act as a plinth to the station building and have been designed to serve as seating steps.
The Lime Street Gateway represents a first phase of public realm improvements to this part of the World Heritage Site. Major changes will follow, allowing the heritage assets more 'breathing' space from traffic as well as improving connections.

IN NEED OF ATTENTION

St John's Gardens are a rare and valuable green space in the centre of the city and are well maintained, as evidenced by the regular award of the national benchmark 'Green Flag' status for parks and open spaces. Many of the historic sculptures within the gardens, however, are suffering from the effects of time and environmental pollution and are in need of careful conservation. The City Council has undertaken an inventory of the monuments, and established a prioritised programme of work, which has begun with laser cleaning and conservation of the Cenotaph. Severe financial constraints have significantly slowed down the programme of conservation.

LOWER DUKE STREET
MERCHANTS QUARTER

Bluecoat St Georges Day 1783

Duke Street lies inland from the Albert Dock, immediately to the south of the city centre. The area developed with merchants' houses and warehouses serving the Old Dock and other early docks. When the historic docks became obsolete in the 20th century, the area fell into steep decline. As a result of concerted efforts and prolonged financial investment on the part of English Heritage, Liverpool City Council and the Heritage Lottery Fund, the area is now a prime example of urban regeneration in progress. To give the wider area a new identity, it was renamed RopeWalks after the long straight yards and streets where rope was made during the 18th century and which still influence the urban grain. The World Heritage Site encompasses the most historically significant parts of RopeWalks, although the whole of the area is of historic interest.

With a couple of notable exceptions, the buildings of this character area are much smaller in scale and less grand than the other parts of the WHS but it represents a crucial stage in the development of the historic port city. The Bluecoat (1717), the oldest surviving building in Liverpool city centre and now a creative hub, was an ambitious project and retains its 18th century character to a high degree. At the east of the area on Colquitt Street, the former Liverpool Royal Institution (1799), originally built as the town mansion for Thomas Parr, together with the adjoining warehouse, is now used as offices and a popular night-time venue.

Liver Bird on overthrow at entrance to The Bluecoat

HISTORY

Before the infilling of the tidal Pool of Liverpool and the construction of Old Dock in 1715, the area now occupied by Duke Street was isolated from the town by the inlet and was an undeveloped heath or common. A plan of 1670 shows that a road in the position of Duke Street ran from the Pool northwards to Quarry Hill, leading to the quarry at St James Mount (now St James Gardens). The opening of the Old Dock heralded the beginning of Liverpool's rise to become an international seaport. This ground-breaking port facility created new opportunities for the merchants of the town and led to demand for land near to the dock and its Custom House for the construction of warehouses and dwellings. The development of the Duke Street area thus represents the first speculative boom in Liverpool. Hanover Street, Duke Street, Fleet Street and Paradise Street were laid out soon after the dock was opened and the Bluecoat was constructed as a school at roughly the same time.

The Charles Eyes plan of 1765 illustrates that within 50 years, the area had been substantially developed, with Wolstenholme Square, Cleveland Square, and connecting streets such as Gradwell Street and Manesty's Lane were all in place. A hierarchy was established, with the broadest streets containing the merchants' houses and shops, and the interconnecting and narrower streets to the rear containing the warehousing and poorer dwellings.

The earliest surviving trade directory for Liverpool, produced by J Gore in 1766, records the population mix. In Cleveland Square, there were nine sea captains, six traders as well as artisans and professionals. Originally the goods brought into the dock were stored in the merchants' houses, but as trade grew, these proved to be inadequate, and private warehouses were constructed adjacent to the houses. Due to the huge demand for plots, the new industrial and warehouse buildings took the form of deep plans front to rear, with narrow street frontages and they were extended in height to four stories or more with a basement.

There was a range of house types from grand Georgian town houses such as Thomas Parr's house to terraces, as seen at 15-25 Duke Street. The squares and gardens and the Ladies Walk along Duke Street demonstrate a desire for a planned and sophisticated expansion of the town. As the warehousing and industrial uses of the area grew during the 19th century, the wealthier merchants relocated to more salubrious suburbs that were being developed higher up the hill in the Rodney Street and Canning Street area and more distant places such

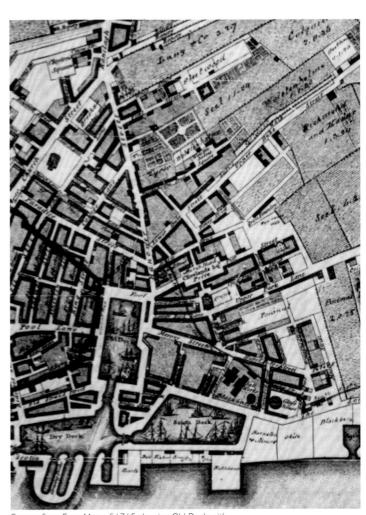

Extract from Eyes Map of 1765 showing Old Dock with Lower Duke Street area at the top right

as Mossley Hill. Some former residential properties were adapted to other uses, with ground floors converted to shops, especially on Bold Street. As part of this process, the area also saw an increase in the number of dock workers, sailors and migrants attracted to the port and its trades, and the accommodation for this group was provided in much poorer back-to-back housing such as Dukes Terrace (1836-1848) just outside the World Heritage Site, and insanitary housing courts (of which no examples survive).

Some cultural activities were established in the area, with the opening of the Union Newsroom (circa 1800) at 105 Duke Street which became Liverpool's first Public Library from 1852 – 60, and the conversion of Thomas Parr's house into the Royal Institution from 1815, dedicated to the promotion of literature, science and the arts.

Early 19th century view of Foster's great Customs House (demolished post-war following WWII bomb damage seen across Canning Dock)

As more docks were constructed in the later 18th century, the Old Dock became separated from the river and was infilled in 1826 to form the site of a colossal new Custom House by John Foster Jnr, which remained a major focal point until it was damaged by bombing during the Second World War and subsequently demolished.

The opening of the Liverpool and Manchester Railway in September 1830 increased the prosperity of the city and was followed by more warehouse building in the area during the later 19th century. These included some of the larger inland ones around Henry Street (33 Argyle Street/14-18 Henry Street). With the introduction of transatlantic steamships in 1840, Liverpool also became a major embarkation point for emigrants seeking their fortunes in the New World, and with its location close to the docks, the Duke Street area attracted boarding houses and settlement of different ethnic groups. The first Chinese community in Europe was established along Nelson Street at the top of Duke Street.

Although Bold Street continues to prosper as a retail thoroughfare, the maritime industry of the Duke Street area went into decline in the 20th century with the closure of the adjacent historic docks and the lack of demand for warehouse space in smaller warehouses. Inevitably, this resulted in the abandonment of historic buildings and in some cases their replacement with newer developments. However, much of the historic fabric survived because of the lack of comprehensive re-development, albeit in a state of extreme dereliction and vacancy. Towards the end of the 20th century, the historic character of the area and low land values attracted artists and craftsmen to establish studios, workshops, galleries and attendant social facilities of bars and restaurants.

Derelict condition of warehouses in Henry St 1990s

By historical accident, Liverpool City Council owned the freehold to most of the land and as leases expired, it became responsible for the maintaining the historic buildings. Although it recognised the need for a comprehensive programme of conservation, it did not have the capacity to undertake it. The Council therefore sold its interest to a developer in the 1980s on the understanding that it would invest heavily in the regeneration of the area and its conservation. Sporadic improvements were made, but the developer soon went bankrupt and it fell to the Council to take the initiative. This it did, with the designation of the Duke Street Conservation Area in 1988 and over time a series of notable projects have been implemented to revitalise the area and conserve its historic fabric. Through the RopeWalks Partnership in the 1980s and 1990s there was massive investment in the resurfacing the streets with traditional materials, training

Bluecoat

© Ian Lawson

programmes were introduced, and area-based conservation schemes have secured the restoration of many historic buildings. During the early 21st century, the area continues to evolve, becoming increasingly a night-time destination with many bars and clubs, as well as increasing numbers of apartments. Following the area's inclusion in the World Heritage Site, a public pot of £4.6million has been established to fund the repair of historic buildings, with contributions from Liverpool City Council, English Heritage, the Heritage Lottery Fund and the (now disbanded) North West Regional Development Agency. This is slowly helping the rejuvenation of the area but the parlous state of many historic buildings means that some difficult decisions still have to be made about whether they can or should be saved. The Liverpool One Development on the west boundary of the area has provided further investment, and involved the restoration of buildings such as Church House, Hanover Street, which has increased confidence that regeneration of the area will eventually be completed.

HIGHLIGHTS

The Bluecoat (1717)
on School Lane was built by Bryan Blundell, a sea captain and merchant, as a residential charity school. It was founded for 'the promotion of Christian charity and the training of poor boys in the principles of the Anglican Church 1717', as expressed in the Latin inscription above the main entrance. The Common Council donated the land, making it the combined product of religious charity, philanthropy and municipal assistance. The school had 50 children by 1719, 46 boys and 16 girls in 1739, 70 children in 1742 and had grown to 375 children by 1800. Thirty six almshouses were added in 1723 at the rear but were demolished (probably in the early-19th century). The Bluecoat School remained in the building until 1906, when it relocated to much larger premises in Wavertree, a Liverpool suburb.

The building was then used by the Sandon Studios Society of Arts, where in 1908 was held the first exhibition outside London of the work of the artist Claude Monet. However, its future was in doubt until 1910 when the Society persuaded the first Lord Leverhulme (who had made his fortune as a soap manufacturer) to buy the building to ensure its continued use as a centre for the arts. In 1911, it hosted the first post-impressionist exhibition with works by international artists including Picasso, Gauguin, Matisse, van Gogh and Cezanne. For a while it also became the home of Liverpool University's School of

Architecture, headed by Charles Reilly who commented '... what happier use could a beautiful old building be put to than to provide studios for young and enthusiastic artists in the daytime and a place for their revelry at night?'

On the death of Lord Leverhulme in 1925, the Bluecoat Society of Arts was established with a mandate to conserve the building, and to use it for promoting the arts in Liverpool. The Bluecoat Gallery was formally established in 1968, to exhibit work by contemporary artists, and has developed a distinctive and sometimes radical exhibition programme, featuring artists from the local to the international, including exhibitions by Yoko Ono and Captain Beefheart. In March 2008, the arts centre re-opened after a £14 million project of restoration and extension to re-establish its original H plan by Rotterdam architects Biq Architecten and it remains a centre for music, dance, literature, art and performance.

The building is of brick and stone in the Queen Anne style, and originally consisted of a hall and chapel at the centre, with two long wings enclosing a cobbled forecourt. The court is entered from School Lane through a gateway surmounted by a Liver Bird. To the rear a landscaped garden provides a quiet environment, which is an oasis of calm in the busy city centre. The building is topped with a cupola, which is a local landmark in the area.

Despite alterations, extensions and reconstructions, the Bluecoat is remarkable for retaining its early 18th century appearance. It is one of the best buildings in Liverpool to provide testimony to the city's cultural traditions during its growth as an international seaport, demonstrating investment in architectural expression, education, philanthropy and culture.

Thomas Parr's house (1799),
Colquitt Street, is one of the earliest remaining examples of a merchant's house with an ancillary, adjoining warehouse. The warehouse in Parr Street, was erected as a separate building but at the same time as the house. Prior to this, warehouses commonly formed the rear part of the merchant's house. In 1815 the house became the Royal Institution when it fell out of residential use, and has more recently become a complex of offices, bars restaurant and performance space. The five storey warehouse was converted to student accommodation in the 1990s.

The house consists of a three-storey, central block with two storey pavilions to either side, connected to the main building by walls. The projecting Doric porch was added by Edmund Aiken c. 1815. At the time when it was his residence, Thomas Parr boasted that he had the 'finest house, the finest horse and the finest wife in Liverpool'. Later in the 19th century, James Picton partially agreed and said that it is '...one of the best examples extant of the establishment of a first-class Liverpool merchant of the period'.

33 Argyle Street/14-18 Henry Street (1884)
is a relatively late pair of adjoining warehouses illustrating the progression of the warehouse type, in which the functional nature of the building is directly expressed and embellished externally. The four storey warehouses on Henry Street are of brown brick with red and blue brick dressings. They have four big gables to Henry Street, each with full-height recessed loading bays outlined in blue brick and a decorated pointed arch to the head. The warehouses on Argyle Street are of similar height and are of brown with just red brick dressings. The red strip of wall containing each vertical column of windows is recessed slightly, then corbelled out near the top with narrow slit windows to bring it flush with the parapet, creating an appearance of fortification. They are by the architect David Walker and have WBW 1884 cast into the panels at the top of the two loading bays. The floors consist of wide, shallow arched vaults carried on iron flanged beams, supported mid-span by cast iron columns, similar to Jesse Hartley's monumental dockside warehouses. The roof structure consists of light sectioned metal, with tension rods, raking struts and metal laths.

Thomas Parr's house (later the Royal Institution) and the adjacent former warehouse (now student accommodation)

Large warehouse at Argyle Street/York Street

Campbell Square

Former Union News Room(1800), home to Liverpool's first library from 1852, now offices

105 Duke Street (c. 1800) is a fine ashlar building by John Foster Snr. It was originally the Union Newsroom and became Liverpool's first public library in 1852-60. The simple brick structure at the rear was added to house the 13th Earl of Derby's natural history collection and was converted to the office of brewers Peter Walker in the 1860s when the extension on Duke Street was added. The original building had its entrance in the centre bay of Duke Street.

Bridewell (1861) is located at the corner of Argyle Street and Campbell Street. The Police Station and holding cells, or Bridewell as it is known locally, was constructed near the docks and near the main lodging areas for the sailors, as many of them became unruly at times due to excessive drinking after long voyages at sea.

Charles Dickens famously spent some time observing the work of the policemen in this building whilst researching for the story of Mercantile Jack in one of his lesser known works, The Uncommercial Traveller.

The bridewell was built principally to hold drunkards in cells but it has been converted to a public house and restaurant and the cells have been retained, ironically as places where customers can get drunk!

The outer side of the security wall on Campbell Street faces on to Campbell Square which has high quality granite paving, clipped sculptural trees and a modern sculpture, The Seed. The square was created around 2004 from a former surface level car park and is one of most successful areas of public open space, being surrounded by both historic buildings and complementary new buildings. The two historic squares in the area, Wolstenholme Square (1765) and Cleveland Square (mid 18th century) still survive but have lost much of their historic fabric and character.

Warehouse and offices (1863 and 1889), 12 Hanover Street

is a combined office and warehouse building of 1889 fronting the corner of Duke Street and Hanover Street, incorporating an earlier warehouse of 1863 in Argyle Street. It was built for Ellis and Company, shipowners and merchants. The building is notable for its hybrid use and its extravagant frontage by the architect Edmund Kirby. The frontage is faced with red engineering brick and matching terracotta detailing, from the Ruabon Terracotta Works, around the windows and facing the chimneys that rise dramatically high above a balustrade. The rich detailing and the rounded facade makes a theatrical statement in its prominent position at the junction of Hanover Street, Duke Street and Paradise Street.

© English Heritage

12 Hanover Street

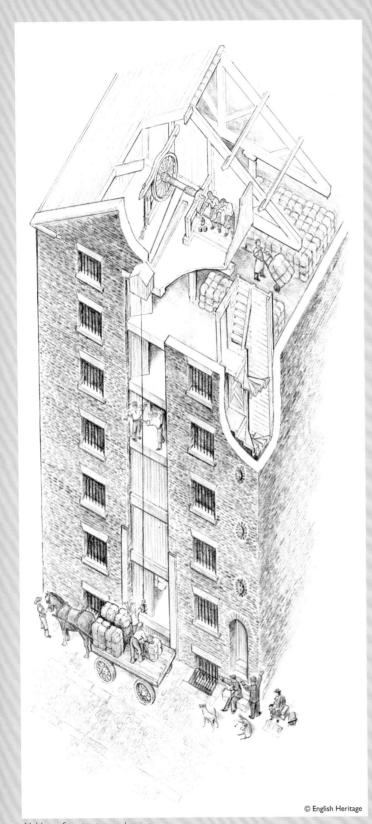

46 Henry Street cutaway drawing

College Lane Warehouses prior to restoration as part of Liverpool One

WAREHOUSES

Warehouses as a building type may seem less impressive than castles, abbeys or mansions but they played a vital role in the development of Liverpool as a port city of global significance. Although buildings such as the Royal Liver Building and St George's Hall are the obvious symbols of Liverpool, the warehouses are just as representative of the city's history. In conjunction with the docks, quaysides and transit sheds, they stored many of the goods that brought prosperity to Liverpool. As testified by the title of English Heritage's 2004 publication Storehouses of Empire, Liverpool's warehouses were essential repositories of trade which was the principal reason for the creation of the British Empire.

A fundamental requirement for a general cargo port is to have safe and suitable storage spaces for the different types of goods that flow through it. The warehouses provided that space but they were built in different sizes and different forms to suit their specific function and they evolved along with changing demands, technology and security requirements. The drawing of Old Dock (on page 4) shows how imported goods were initially simply unloaded on to the quaysides and were thus highly vulnerable to theft. The drawing also shows the second Customs House, directly overlooking the dock, so that the customs officers could try to ensure that they had a proper record of imports.

Monumental dockside warehouses were first introduced in the late 18th century, when the Duke of Bridgewater built a large stone warehouse at Duke's Dock in 1783. This type of warehouse, where the goods could be transferred directly into

42 Fleet Street - a combined house and warehouse

They are typically five or six storeys high, although one in Gradwell Street survives with increased storage space of 8 storeys and a warehouse in Henry Street has only one tall storey.

At least one full-height vertical loading bay with loading doors on every floor was provided on the roadside frontage to enable goods to be hoisted in and out using an overhead pulley, usually protected by a cover called a cathead. These loading bays are the clearest indicator of the original use of the building and

Large Warehouse at the corner of Henry Street and York Street

the warehouses from the ships and could be held until required, was built most impressively during Jesse Hartley's reign as Dock Engineer (1824-60), with the warehouses at Albert Dock, Stanley Dock and Wapping Dock. These were built by the Dock Committee within the Dock Estate, where the Customs Officers could keep closer control of the goods and therefore ensure that the full import taxes were paid. They reached their apogee with the construction of the colossal Tobacco Warehouse (1901) at Stanley Dock which, with 27 million bricks, was the largest brick warehouse in the world - later described as 'the King Kong of Docklands'!

By contrast, private warehouses were distributed throughout the city centre and are especially well represented in the Lower Duke Street Merchants Quarter, which was close to the early docks. In the 18th century, a warehouse was often built on the same plot as the merchant's house. Sometimes the houses and warehouses were actually part of the same building as seen at the corner of Henry Street and York Street, where the domestic element fronts on to York Street and the warehouse element fronts on to Henry Street. A variation on the type is where the warehouses are slightly separate from the house, as seen at Thomas Parr's house and warehouse at Colquitt Street/Parr Street. Another example is the pair of four-storey brick warehouses (late 18th century) at the rear on College Lane, which have been sensitively conserved in the Liverpool One Development, complete with winding gear above the loading bay, and are now used as shops and a restaurant.

The provisions of the 1803 Warehousing Act were extended to Liverpool in 1805 and this established the formation of bonded warehouses, where goods could remain under Crown security until they were sent out of the warehouses, when duty was paid on them. For non-perishable goods and tobacco, which could be left to cure within a warehouse for up to 3 years, this meant that the value and taxes due could change dramatically during their time in bond. Bonds in the goods were bought by a wide range of people across the country and reclaimed when the goods were sold. Most of the bonded warehouses were on the dockside but one was built at 46 Henry Street and an earlier non-bonded warehouse at 38 Henry Street was converted to a bonded warehouses and the size of the windows had to be reduced to enforce security.

Most of the 19th century warehouses in Lower Duke Street were constructed independently from their owner's residence, as the owners had migrated to more fashionable areas up the hill in the Canning Street area. These private inland warehouses typically occupy deep narrow plots with a gabled frontage.

make a strong visual statement. The lifting of goods was a potentially hazardous procedure, for both warehouse workers and passers-by. Risks for workers were reduced by providing temporary safety barriers, built-in handles in the reveals of the loading bays and even securing ropes to the workers' belts. Risks for pedestrians were reduced by recessing the loading bays and doors back from the pavement.

Windows were generally limited to the narrow front elevation due to the tightness of building across the plot and even those were few and small, to prevent theft and the deterioration of perishable goods. Welsh blue slate was almost always used for the roof covering and walls were usually built in common bricks, although later polychromatic bricks and stone dressings were introduced. Early warehouses had timber floors supported by stout timber columns but a series of disastrous fires such as the one at New Quay in 1833 led to a series of changes to warehouse design. In 1842, 140 warehouse fires were recorded, many caused by careless use of lighting due to the darkness of the interior. As a result several local Building Acts were passed by the Liverpool Corrporation to require the provision of thicker walls, metal doors, a fireproof staircase bay, cast iron columns on the ground floor and party walls rising above the roof-line and the use of non-combustible materials for external features. Some merchants went a stage further and used non-combustible materials throughout: this prevented the buildings from catching fire but not necessarily the goods within them.

12 Hanover Street

During the later 19th century, a further form of warehouse evolved, in which a warehouse was constructed in conjunction with either a showroom for display of the goods for sale (more typically in the Castle Street Historic Commercial District) or the office of the importer, as at 12 Hanover Street.

The port of Liverpool now handles more tonnage of goods than ever before but commodities and trade patterns have changed dramatically and almost none of the small inland warehouses in Lower Duke Street area are in use as warehouses. If they are to be retained then they must be adapted to new uses and some interventions in their historic fabric are inevitable. Many examples of successful conversions to apartments, hotels, offices, shops, bars and restaurants in the area demonstrate how this can be achieved.

WHAT THEY SAID

Bryan Blundell early-18th century:

'… on the strength of which I went to work and got the present Charity School built which has cost between two and three hundred pounds and was finished in 1718, at which time I gave for the encouragement of the charity, seven hundred and fifty pounds, being a tenth part of what it pleased God to bless me with, and did then purpose to continue to give the same proportion of whatever He should indulge me with in the time to come for the benefit of the charity.'

Charles Dickens *The Uncommercial Traveller* 1860:

'This was my thought as I walked the dock-quays at Liverpool, keeping watch on poor Mercantile Jack... Mercantile Jack was hard at it in the hard weathers – as he mostly is in most weathers, poor Jack. He was girded to ships' masts and funnels of steamers, like a forester to a great oak, scraping and painting: he was lying out on yards, furling sails that tried to beat him off; he was dimly discernible up in a world of giant cobwebs, reefing and splicing; he was faintly discernable down in its holds, stowing and unshipping cargo; he was winding round and round at capstans melodious monotonous and drunk; he was of diabolical aspect, with coaling for the Antipodes; he was washing decks barefoot, with the breast of his red shirt open to the blast, though it was sharper than the knife in his leathern girdle; he was looking over bullwarks, all eyes and hair; he was standing by at the shoot of the Cunard steamer, off tomorrow, as the stocks in trade of several

butchers, poulterers and fishmongers poured down into the ice-house; he was coming aboard of other vessels, with his kit in a tarpaulin bag, attended by plunderers to the very last moment of his shore-going existence.'

Anon 1820:

'The number and extraordinary magnitude of the warehouses which meet the eye in almost every direction in the vicinity of the docks, are very interesting to a stranger. Their elevation, by which the number of these indispensable receptacles of merchandise is increased upon the quays, and the facility with which goods are hoisted up to the highest stories, entitle them to peculiar notice.'

29 - 35 Seel Street before restoration

HERITAGE ACHIEVEMENTS SINCE INSCRIPTION

The Nadler Hotel, Seel Street

The urban regeneration programme within the RopeWalks in general and the Lower Duke Street Merchants Quarter in particular has included many major achievements. One of the most successful restorations has been The Nadler Hotel, a former industrial building in Seel Street, which is just outside the World Heritage Site. It was built in the 1850s for T & T Vickers & Co, a prestigious engineers and iron founder. From the late-19th century to the mid-20th, the building housed a great variety of small businesses including cork importers and beeswax traders. Between the 1960s and the late 1970s, it became the home to Seel House Press and it was here that Liverpool Football Club's 'Anfield Press' was printed. Programmes from that time covered five league-winning seasons, the club's league and UEFA cup doubles. The building then lay derelict from the late 1970s until 2008 when it was bought for restoration and conversion to an innovative hotel, with 106 bedrooms which has no dining facilities of its own, but each room has small kitchen facilities and the hotel has arrangements with surrounding restaurants to give discount to guests.

The renovation scheme, which received grant assistance, was implemented at a total cost of £14m in 2009-10 and retained the external character and many internal historic features. It also introduced many contemporary elements to create an exciting blend of traditional and modern.

IN NEED OF ATTENTION

In spite of the progress made in conserving the historic Lower Duke Street area, much challenging work remains to be done. Two important terraces of merchants houses which are privately owned and which have received only minimal maintenance during their recent ownership are 118-124 Duke Street and across the road, 151-55 Duke Street. The first, on the south side, is a terrace of fine 3-storey Georgian houses with Doric doorcases. The three houses in the terrace on the north side were larger, with five bays but have been more altered. Both terraces are earlier versions of similar houses further up Upper Duke Street in the Georgian Canning area which itself fell into decline during the mid 20th century but was comprehensively restored at the end of that century during a long programme of investment and care from the City Council, English Heritage and the various building owners. The turnaround in condition of the Canning area demonstrates the potential of these terraces and the tragedy of their continued neglect. Some superficial improvements have been undertaken to both terraces following the threat of action by Liverpool City Council but they remain empty, a blight on the surrounding area and in need of attention.

29 - 35 Seel Street after renovation

Duke Street terrace in need of attention

USING THE
CITY'S PAST TO INFORM
NEW DESIGN

Relationship of the Arena and Conference Centre with the Anglican Cathedral

LIVERPOOL - A MODERN CITY

Liverpool, world heritage status notwithstanding, is not an ancient city with a legacy of continuous development going back to the classical era. Whilst archaeological evidence illustrates that there was some activity in Roman times, and earlier, it is not a York or a Chester. Even though it received its Charter in 1207, nothing remains of medieval Liverpool apart from the location of the original seven streets, from where the city expanded.

The crucial event that was the catalyst for the extraordinary leap in the fortunes of Liverpool, was the opening of the Old Dock of 1715, a massive undertaking and risk, and a speculative act of faith. The exponential growth in maritime trade and physical expansion from this time led to the city we recognise. The morphology, buildings and townscape that we encounter today are the result of Liverpool's progression from 1715 onwards – in historic terms, this is a modern city.

Born of risk, purposefulness, commercial expediency, innovation and sheer single-minded determination, Liverpool has a distinctive character that is unlike anywhere else. It is decidedly not a genteel, reserved place, but confident, brash, frequently ostentatious and often 'edgy'. In addition to financial and commercial activities, the main currency is that of ideas. Invention, adaptation, re-definition – taking a concept and providing a peculiar Liverpool 'twist' – is a key element in Liverpool's cultural heritage, whether that be in commerce, poetry, music or architecture.

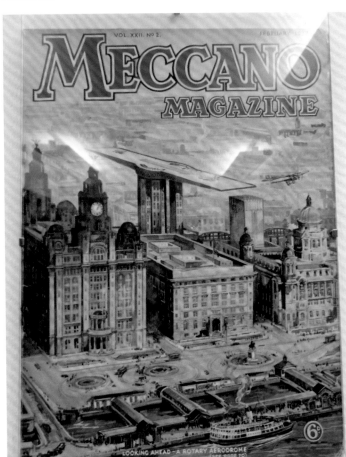

Cover of Meccano Magazine from 1930s: Liverpool's Waterfront "Looking Ahead - A Rotary Aerodrome"!

These traits have often been manifest in the response to its new buildings. In Peter Ellis' Oriel Chambers of 1864 for example, Liverpool is a forerunner in the development of modern building technology. Bold and radical for its time, it influenced the firm of Burnham and Root in the design of tall buildings in 19th century Chicago. Yet it was castigated in the architectural press. Liverpool's totemic symbol, the Liver Building, completed in 1911, was in turn inspired by contemporary American design, and was hailed as Europe's first skyscraper. But it was considered brutal and inappropriate for the site when it was constructed. The Three Graces at Pier Head were criticised as 'one of the best, or worst, examples of excessive individualism in architecture'. Even the mannered and now much-admired Neo-classical St George's Hall of 1854, designed by the 25-year old Harvey Lonsdale Elmes, was mired in controversy at the outset. Similar heated discussions took place concerning both the Anglican and Metropolitan Cathedrals.

Liverpool has a long tradition of ambivalence to new design, a dual approach to encouraging the memorable and dynamic, but coupled with criticism and opprobrium. It is as if when faced with radical developments that embody the progressive spirit and characteristics of the city itself, there is sometimes a loss of self-confidence both from within the city and outside.

New design and its contribution to the city's past

Since World Heritage Site inscription in 2004, a further layer of design assessment has been added. Do the new developments take account of the 'outstanding universal values' of the site? How do they fit with the city's distinctive urban character? Do they conform to the unique legacy of historic buildings and spaces that define the city? A brief description of some of the high profile new developments within the World Heritage Site and its buffer zone illustrates how new design can shape the city's future identity.

Since the late 1990's, a key strategy has been to re-connect the city centre to the waterfront, and to maximise connections elsewhere, so that the city is legible and easy to navigate. Regenerating the waterfront and reclaiming the River Mersey as an asset for the city has been central to this strategy. Paving all principal streets and public spaces with a simple palette of materials based on granite and sandstone has provided the 'glue' that helps unite the different character areas. Opportunities have been taken to make some of these spaces dynamic and flexible. The Pier Head piazza at the heart of the World Heritage Site, for example, has not just been adapted, but a waterway has been extended through it, providing an extra element and opening up the route between the Leeds and Liverpool Canal and the historic docks. The Pier Head is also a gateway for the Mersey Ferry service that crosses the river, and the nearby cruise liner facility. The river that carried so much cargo, both goods and migrants, and where the great transatlantic liners started their voyages in the 20th century, had seen its shipping activity reduced to almost nothing. With the re-shaping of the Pier Head, and the construction of a facility to the north, the great ships have returned, and although they now carry tourists instead of migrants, the cruise liners that berth near to the Port of Liverpool Building, the Cunard Building and the Liver Building, have restored a sense of scale and activity not seen in five decades.

New development such as the Museum of Liverpool and the Mann Island buildings were the result of a masterplan that involved a careful assessment of key views in the area, and a historical analysis of the waterfront. The Museum of Liverpool was designed to work with the new canal and basin, and to extend the Pier Head public realm into and through the building. The external steps that give access to the first floor provide a higher vantage point that brings a different perspective to the river and the Albert Dock, and these new views are complemented by the massive windows comprising the north and south elevations that provide panoramic views of the Three Graces, the canal and the

Museum of Liverpool

Mann Island seen from Albert Dock

river, so that the city itself becomes part of the Museum exhibit. The plan form of the building, based around a central spiral staircase, marks the point of entrance to the former Manchester Dock. Its alignment takes its cue from the nearby Canning Dry Docks, which also mark the channel that early ships used to enter the tidal creek from the Mersey.

The Mann Island development was designed as a group of three buildings rather than as a continuation of the Three Graces, and the blocks are intended to be seen as floating objects, cast adrift in the black waters of the dock, which their black granite elevations reflect. The forms of the buildings and their composition are also inspired by the history of the docks. For when these docks were in commercial use, there was always something in the viewing field. Buildings, ships, overhead railways – all these at one time or another allowed only glimpsed views of the Three Graces from the south.

In developing the masterplan for Liverpool One, the opportunity was also taken to celebrate the World Heritage Site and the city's evolution. The project was designed to re-connect the various areas of the city and re-establish routes that had been severed or downgraded. There are new links leading to the historically important RopeWalks area of early merchants' houses and warehousing, and also upgraded connections to the commercial quarter. The area that is adjacent to RopeWalks has narrow streets and prominent buildings that relate to the grain of the area and help with navigation. Small details, such as the view of the cupola of Bluecoat Chambers from Paradise Street, have been highlighted and act as landmarks. The elliptical buildings that embrace Chavasse Park create a framed view of the Albert Dock, and emphasise the connections between Liverpool One and the waterfront.

The major axis to the waterfront along the southern side of Chavasse Park was chosen as it was the location of the Old Dock. The dock itself was excavated as part of the project, and has been consolidated and preserved beneath the street. The area of the dock is marked in the paving, and the water features – consisting of an interlinked series of pools and fountains – celebrate its location. The park has been planted with native species that would have been prevalent at that time, such as birch, and the red sandstone outcropping has been used for retaining walls.

Other buildings symbolise the later history of the World Heritage Site and its importance, not just as a trading port, but also as a destination for Atlantic convoys in the Second World War. The Unity development at 20 Chapel Street is one of the new series of towers constructed since 2000. The cladding scheme and the use of the distinctive 'ships-bridge' penthouses were inspired by the 'dazzle' ships that were a feature of the wartime transatlantic trade. For the strong geometric painting of convoy escort Royal Navy and merchant shipping, developed from Vorticist art, was used so that the hulls and superstructures of ships were broken down to confuse enemy U-boats. This Dazzle-ship motif is used to create a series of rhythms on the elevations of the new towers.

Similarly, the Arena and Conference Centre at Kings Dock has the look and feel of a ship moored in the Mersey. South of the grade I listed Albert Dock, the building was designed to follow through with the height of the warehouses, adding to the long horizontal axis that is a feature of this part of the World Heritage Site and its buffer zone. The curved roofs and central atrium suggest the wings and body of a seagull in flight to some, of a swimmer to others, but the grey tones and strength of the simple plan form and façade treatment are

© Rob Burns

Unity development at 20 Chapel Street with St Nicholas Church

also strongly reminiscent of the hull of a large ship such as the aircraft carrier Ark Royal, built across the Mersey at Cammell Lairds. The current extension to provide further exhibition halls continues the simple aesthetic of the Arena.

The massive investment made since 2000 to improve public spaces has delivered great benefits. Within the RopeWalks the streetscape has been transformed to encourage further investment, and a series of new pocket parks has been opened. Important streets such as Castle Street have been re-paved and traffic management introduced to encourage pedestrian movement and activity on the street. One of the main schemes has been the new entrance to Lime Street Station, which celebrates the world's first commercial railway line built in 1830 between Liverpool and Manchester, and provides a fitting welcome to the city.

The Lime Street gateway scheme represents a first phase of improvements to this part of the World Heritage Site, which is planned to become a hub and events space for the city. Future changes will reduce the impact of through traffic, allowing Lime Street and St George's Plateau to be used for festivals and gatherings. Connections between the William Brown Street cultural quarter and the rest of the city centre will be enhanced, and the setting of the major public buildings will be improved. Other street works and pedestrian schemes will improve access to the waterfront across The Strand, providing better links between the different character areas of the World Heritage Site.

New design and the future

The most controversial and largest regeneration opportunity for the city is the Liverpool Waters scheme, partially located in the World Heritage Site. Stretching north from Princes Dock, and covering 60 hectares of redundant dockland, the project was given outline permission in 2013. But it poses major challenges. English Heritage and UNESCO believe that if the extent of development

permitted were built, it would be so dominant in the cityscape that Liverpool's value as 'the supreme example of a commercial port at the time of Britain's greatest global influenced' could be harmed, and the issue has led to Liverpool being placed on UNESCO'S list of World Heritage in Danger.

The scheme is intended to be phased over a 30-year period, and building work will only start after completion of a series of detailed masterplans and design studies, with further economic development being undertaken by the site owners, Peel Holdings. The project has been divided into a series of distinct neighbourhoods, and as well as buildings it contains substantial areas of water in the docks and two new parks. Comprising office, residential, leisure, hotel and entertainment uses, the proposals will open up a redundant and formerly private area of the waterfront. All the historic structures on the site, such as the Victoria Clock Tower, will be restored and re-used, and the remnants of the historic floorscape such as granite setts and quayside capstans will be retained. Peel Holdings and Liverpool City Council are appointing two independent panels to give advice on design and heritage issues as the scheme progresses, including representatives from English Heritage.

All parties are determined to see Liverpool removed from the World Heritage In Danger list, and are working together to ensure this happens. The objective must be to build in a manner that does not overwhelm the historic port, that protects the archaeological evidence for the historic docks, and commits to the highest design standards that reflect the spirit of the place. For Liverpool's urban landscape sets a very high benchmark that demands the most thoughtful and rigorous approach to planning and architectural excellence. This is a tough call, but to do the right thing by Liverpool is an obligation which cannot be avoided, and if this can be achieved, the city, its people, its economy, and the development community will all benefit. That is the central challenge for the future of the World Heritage Site.

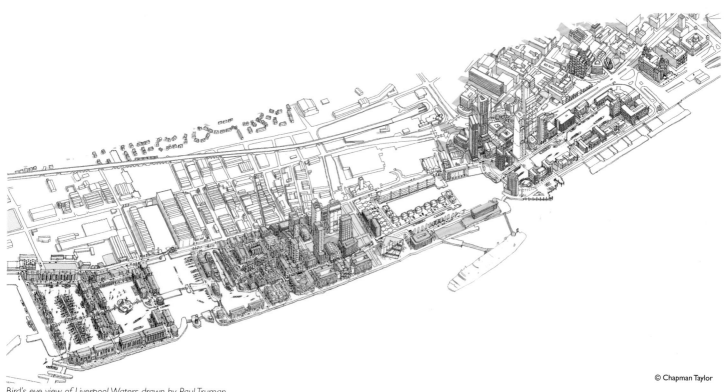

© Chapman Taylor

Bird's eye view of Liverpool Waters drawn by Paul Truman

LIVERPOOL MARITIME MERCANTILE CITY WORLD HERITAGE SITE

Statement of Outstanding Universal Value

Brief Description

The Maritime Mercantile City of Liverpool became one of the centres of world trade in the 18th and 19th centuries. It had an important role in the growth of the British Empire and became the major port for the mass movement of people, especially enslaved Africans and European emigrants. Liverpool pioneered the development of modern dock technology, transport systems, port management, and building construction. A series of significant commercial, civic and public buildings lie within selected areas in the historic docklands and the centre of the city. These areas include: the Pier Head, with its three principal waterfront buildings – the Royal Liver Building, the Cunard Building and the Port of Liverpool Building; the Dock area with their warehouses, dock walls, docks and other facilities related to port activities from the 18th and 19th centuries; the mercantile area, with its shipping offices, produce exchanges, marine insurance offices, banks, inland warehouses and merchants houses; and the William Brown Street Cultural Quarter, including St George's Plateau, with its monumental cultural and civic buildings.

Statement of Significance

Liverpool – Maritime Mercantile City reflects the role of Liverpool as the supreme example of a commercial port at the time of Britain's greatest global influence. Liverpool grew into a major commercial port in the 18th century, when it was also crucial for the organisation of the trans-Atlantic slave trade. In the 19th century, Liverpool became a world mercantile centre for general cargo and mass European emigration to the New World. It had major significance on world trade being one of the principal ports of the British Commonwealth. Its innovative techniques and types of construction of dock facilities became an important reference worldwide. Liverpool also became instrumental in the development of industrial canals in the British Isles in the 18th century, as well as of railway transport in the 19th century. All through this period, and particularly in the 19th and early 20th centuries, Liverpool gave attention to the quality and innovation of its architecture and cultural activities. To this stand as testimony its outstanding public buildings, such as St George's Hall and its museums. Even in the 20th century, Liverpool has given a lasting contribution, which is remembered in the success of The Beatles.

Criteria for Inscription

Criterion (ii): Liverpool was a major centre generating innovative technologies and methods in dock construction and port management in the 18th, 19th and early 20th centuries. It thus contributed to the building up of the international mercantile systems throughout the British Commonwealth.

Criterion (iii): the city and the port of Liverpool are an exceptional testimony to the development of maritime mercantile culture in the 18th, 19th and early 20th centuries, contributing to the building up of the British Empire. It was a centre for the slave trade, until its abolition in 1807, and for emigration from northern Europe to America.

Criterion (iv): Liverpool is an outstanding example of a world mercantile port city, which represents the early development of global trading and cultural connections throughout the British Empire.

Assessment of the Conditions of Authenticity and Integrity, and of the Requirements for Protection and Management in Force

Integrity

The existing urban fabric of the World Heritage Site dates from the 18th to the 20th centuries, with an emphasis on the 19th and early 20th centuries. The city has suffered from the Second World War destruction as well as from the long economic decline after the war.

The historic evolution of the Liverpool street pattern is still readable representing the different periods. There have been some alterations after the war destruction in 1941.

Judging in the overall, though, the protected area has well retained its historic integrity. Not only are the buildings in good state but every effort has been made to preserve the minor detailing of architecture such as the original pulleys of the docks and various other cast iron features.

Authenticity

In the World Heritage property, the main historic buildings have retained their authenticity to a high degree. There are a small number of areas, especially in the buffer zone, where the damages from the war period still exist. There are also new constructions from the second half of the 20th century, of which not all are to high standard. The main docks survive as water-filled basins within the World Heritage property and the buffer zone. They are not any more operational, though one dock area is operated by Merseyside Maritime Museum, and another is used for ship repairs. The warehouses are being converted to new uses. Here attention is given to keep changes to the minimum.

Protection and Management

The World Heritage Site is within the boundary of Liverpool City Council. The property is protected through the planning system and through the designation of over 260 buildings. The whole property is protected by Conservation Areas.

The World Heritage Site is subject to different plans and policies, including the Liverpool Unitary Development Plan (2002), the Strategic Regeneration Framework (July 2001) and the Liverpool Maritime Mercantile City World Heritage Site SPD (2009). There are several detailed master plans for specified areas, and conservation plans for the individual buildings. A full Management Plan has been prepared for the World Heritage Site. Its implementation is overseen by a Liverpool World Heritage Site Steering Group, which includes most public bodies involved in the property.

UNITED NATIONS EDUCATIONAL,
SCIENTIFIC AND
CULTURAL ORGANIZATION

CONVENTION CONCERNING
THE PROTECTION OF THE WORLD
CULTURAL AND NATURAL
HERITAGE

The World Heritage Committee
has inscribed

Liverpool - Maritime Mercantile City

on the World Heritage List

Inscription on this List confirms the exceptional
and universal value of a cultural or
natural site which requires protection for the benefit
of all humanity

DATE OF INSCRIPTION

7 July 2004

DIRECTOR-GENERAL
OF UNESCO

BIBLIOGRAPHY

Belchem J, Merseypride, 2000

Belchem J, (ed), Liverpool 800: Culture, Character & History, 2006

Bluecoat Press, Liverpool Images of a great seaport, 1992

Brown S and de Figueiredo P, Religion and Place: Liverpool's historic places of worship, 2008

Burton V (ed), Liverpool Shipping, Trade and Industry, 1989

Cavanagh T, Public Sculpture of Liverpool, 1997

City of Liverpool, Liverpool Maritime Mercantile City: Nomination Document, 2003

City of Liverpool, Liverpool Maritime Mercantile City: Management Plan, 2003

Cossons N and Jenkins M, Liverpool: Seaport City, 2011

Ferneyhough F, Liverpool and Manchester Railway 1830-1980, 1980

Giles C, Building a Better Society: Liverpool's historic institutional buildings, 2008

Giles C and Hawkins R, Storehouses of Empire: Liverpool's historic warehouses, 2004

Hughes Q, Seaport, 1964

Hughes Q, Liverpool: City of Architecture, 1999

Hyde F E, Liverpool and the Mersey, 1971

Jarvis A, Liverpool Central Docks 1799-1905, 1991

Jarvis A, The Liverpool Dock Engineers, 1996

Lane T, Liverpool: city of the sea, 1997

Muir, R, A History of Liverpool, 1907

Picton J A, Memorials of Liverpool, 1873

Ritchie-Noakes N, Liverpool's Historic Waterfront, 1984

Sharples J, Liverpool (Pevsner Architectural Guides), 2004

Sharples J and Stonard J, Built on Commerce: Liverpool's central business district, 2008

Tanner M, Merseyside Maritime Museum – The Ship and Boat Collection, 1995

Tibbles A, Merseyside Maritime Museum Illustrated Catalogue of Marine Paintings, 1999

ACKNOWLEDGEMENTS AND THANKS

The initiative to produce this book was taken by the directors of Peel Holdings, who assembled a team of authors and designers; and secured sponsorship from other companies and organisations with a passion for Liverpool's heritage to make it possible.

Sponsors:
Liverpool City Council
Peel Holdings
English Heritage
Liverpool One
Broadway Malyan
Gower Street Estates (Albert Dock) Ltd.
Harcourt Developments
The Liverpool Waterfront Business Partnership CIC
Planit -IE LLP

Editor:
Peter de Figueiredo

Authors:
Professor Ian Wray
John Hinchliffe
Peter de Figueiredo
Rob Burns

Photography and illustrations:
English Heritage
National Museums Liverpool
Walker Art Gallery
Liverpool Record Office
Liverpool City Council
National Trust
Canal and River Trust
Peel Ports
Paula Graham
John Benbow
John Hinchliffe
Rob Burns
John 'Hoppy' Hopkins

The following are also thanked for their help:
Sir Neil Cossons
Karl Creaser
Catherine Downey
David Stoker
Anne Gleave
Martin Bailey
Julian Treuherz
Lesley Woodbridge

Design:
Planit-IE LLP
www.planit-ie.com

Printed by W&G Baird, Northern Ireland

PUBLISHED BY BLUECOAT PRESS, LIVERPOOL